GHOSTS AND LEGENDS OF
FLORIDA PIRATES

HEATHER LEIGH, PhD

Haunted
America

Published by Haunted America
A Division of The History Press
Charleston, SC
www.historypress.com

First published 2024

Manufactured in the United States

ISBN 9781467156912

Library of Congress Control Number: 2024937572

Notice: The information in this book is true and complete to the best of our knowledge. It is offered without guarantee on the part of the author or The History Press. The author and The History Press disclaim all liability in connection with the use of this book.

*Dedicated to the memory of my beloved grandmother
Florence Geeraerts (Pattyn), 1914–1981, whose unwavering belief
in my potential and endless encouragement fueled my dreams.
Your legacy of love and support continues to inspire me every day.
Thank you for teaching me to dream big.*

CONTENTS

CONTENTS

FOREWORD

Pirates captivate our imaginations. *The Black Pirate* (1926) starring Douglas Fairbanks Sr. romanticized the swashbuckling villain and catapulted the iconic themes of pillaging and plundering into the action-adventure genre. This silent film showcased how motion picture audiences suspended their moral compass to root for the handsome, sword-carrying buccaneers whose adventures and conquests comprised the Golden Age of Hollywood. However, the travelers on the high seas were not, in fact, men—and sometimes a few women—to aspire to become. No, their legacies were fraught with savagery.

Journey around the coastal areas of Florida, and you will hear legends of men who viciously attacked towns and robbed vessels, searching for that elusive treasure chest of bullion. While the fictional Spanish buccaneer José Gaspar inspired Tampa's annual Ye Mystic Crew of Gasparilla, most pirates are not celebrated. However, they are studied to determine whether their negative life energy scarred the very coastal towns they terrorized.

Ghosts and Legends of Florida Pirates presents a compelling argument that these pirates may be haunting various towns across the Sunshine State. While other books and blogs focus on the Atlantic coast of Florida, Heather Leigh's book includes important locations on the Gulf of Mexico. And she doesn't stop at pirate biographies and town lore.

Heather Leigh delves deeper into additional paranormal hot spots, including lighthouses and shipwrecks. She reminds us that paranormal activity is not isolated to dry land.

Florida is special. There are still plenty of unspoiled environmentally important areas where a small sloop could easily navigate the narrow waterways back in the pirate era. Try to visualize them when reading about Cedar Key and Seahorse Key.

Admittedly, I'm a fan of Heather Leigh's work, whether in print or online through Ghost Education 101. As a researcher, I appreciate the candor and honesty she brings to the paranormal community. She works diligently, proffering a unique perspective through her inclusion of non–tourist trap destinations. Heather Leigh offers additional stories that are underrepresented in the usual ghost tour spiel that we all have heard. Her approach to this book was to include the offshore legends and destinations that may not have been on your radar. As a native Floridian, I'm thrilled to see some of these stories finally emerge in print.

Equal to her researching is Heather Leigh's writing. She excels at capturing the American landscape that makes our country special whether she is retelling ghost stories from abandoned ghost towns of Nevada or the turbulent high seas off the coast of Florida. *Ghosts and Legends of Florida Pirates* provides the destinations for your road trip, as well as crafting the characters for your epic adventure. Grab a life jacket. You will definitely want to charter a boat to experience fully these beautiful, historic and unique swashbuckling locales.

Lesia Miller Schnur
The Haunted Librarian

ACKNOWLEDGEMENTS

As always, I am eternally grateful for the love and support of my family and enjoy having them join me on my paranormal adventures. Josh and Aidan, there are many more adventures to come.

Thank you, Lesia Miller Schnur, The Haunted Librarian, for writing a fantastic foreword. I look forward to having you back on Ghost Education 101 again soon and working on future research projects together.

Thank you (again), Philip R. Wyatt, my co-host of Ghost Education 101, for letting me use your fantastic photos of the St. Augustine Lighthouse. We need to investigate together soon!

INTRODUCTION

Surrounded on three sides by water, Florida has always been a beacon for seafaring explorers. Ever since Ponce de León arrived on the Sunshine State's shores in 1513, the state has quickly grown, becoming a place for pirates to live, conquer, laugh, love, pillage, hide and bury their beloved treasure.

Cities such as St. Augustine provided seafaring explorers with vibrant seaports, and Spanish vessels were among the first to stop in Florida. Florida and its many small islands were vital stops for sea travelers to get supplies and take a break from braving the ocean waters for extended periods.

Pirates worldwide discovered that Florida was a popular destination for these vessels and quickly made their way to the Caribbean, the Gulf of Mexico and Florida's coastal waters of the Atlantic Ocean. Their goal was to attack the many vessels stopping during their long journeys, and over time, the state became a hub for some of the most feared and dangerous pirates throughout history.

The Golden Era of Piracy in Florida and throughout the Gulf of Mexico was between 1650 and 1730. Though piracy dwindled after 1730, another spike occurred during the Revolutionary War in the late 1700s and continued through the early 1800s. During these times, pirates pillaged ships and profited from smuggling, bringing goods to sell and trade in the American ports that were once being blocked by the British navy.

Left: This statue of Ponce de León stands proudly in St. Augustine. *Library of Congress, Carol M. Highsmith.*

Right: Portrait of Sir Francis Drake. *Library of Congress.*

Legendary pirates, such as Sir Francis Drake, Blackbeard, Captain Kidd, Black Caesar, José Gaspar and more, were known throughout the state. As warships made their way to Florida, many pirates hid, never to be seen again. Others escaped, heading to other coastal areas where they could continue their pirate lifestyle. Many more were captured and hanged for acts of piracy.

Regardless of what happened to the pirates of Florida, their legends continue. Residents share stories, visitors come to experience pirate-like activities and the state is home to one of the largest pirate festivals in the country.

Florida definitely holds the key to pirate life, which could explain why many of the spirits of the most famous and feared pirates are still seen today. Whether you are walking the streets of St. Augustine or exploring Key West, chances are you will come face-to-face with one of the pirates who still call Florida home.

1

WERE THERE MANY PIRATES IN FLORIDA?

Florida provided pirates the perfect world and location to live the stereotypical pirate lifestyle. With water on three sides, the state was a popular destination for seafarers and ocean vessels to stop for a break. Florida's weather is ideal for vessels to dock and travelers to establish a new life in the Sunshine State, and pirates recognized the continued flow of new people and opportunities as a way to get rich through attacking, pillaging and kidnapping.

With water all around the state, coral reefs just offshore and dangerously dark shorelines, many ships wrecked in Florida's coastal waters. These shipwrecks provided easy pickings for pirates to paddle out and collect treasure, such as gold, emeralds, rubies, topaz, pearls, ivory, turquoise and more. Additionally, when pirates wanted to hide their treasure or themselves, Florida was overgrown with vast amounts of wilderness, creating the perfect cover to keep their secrets.

As Florida's coastline was mapped out, pirates started to better understand the state and its potential piracy hot spots. New maps gave them a guide to create plans and turn being a pirate into a lucrative profession.

Piracy became more profitable with less work; even noblemen, including Ponce de León, changed professions, becoming pirates of the high seas. Though de León was a Spanish governor and credited with discovering Florida, he was attracted to exploring. He eventually became greedy as he pillaged and plundered the areas he explored. Then he suddenly had his heart set on finding the Fountain of Youth and all the gold he could collect along the way.

Left: An actual pirate treasure chest sits on display at the St. Augustine Pirate and Treasure Museum. *Library of Congress, Carol M. Highsmith.*

Below: Costumed participants enjoying the adventures during the annual Gasparilla Festival in Tampa. *Library of Congress, Karl E. Holland.*

A rough estimate claims more than five thousand pirates roamed Florida's coastline between the peak years of 1715 and 1735. Some of the most successful and feared pirates of the Caribbean known to operate in Florida included Henry Avery, Anne Bonny, Captain Henry Morgan, John "Calico Jack" Rackham, Mary Reed, Robert Searle and Charles Vane.

Real-life pirates flocked to Florida, the Gulf of Mexico and the Caribbean Sea. These violent thieves were desperate to avoid being captured, and they would torture and murder anyone who posed a risk to their lifestyle. Though a pirate's career was not long-lived, there was no shortage of replacements waiting to be the most feared and profitable pirate.

Map of Florida. *New York Public Library.*

2

WHY DID PIRATES LIKE FLORIDA?

Once Florida became a key stopping place for Spanish vessels, the state quickly became irresistible to pirates. Pirates were drawn to the state because the stopovers of these vessels made them easy to attack and provided them with a near-infinite supply of treasure.

The Florida Keys became a staging point for Spanish treasure ships preparing to voyage home to Spain from Havana. News of what vessels docked in the keys quickly spread, and pirates soon found that the southernmost tip of Florida was perfect for staging ambushes within the many straits and passages of the keys.

Beyond the Florida Keys, much of the Gulf Coast of Florida had inlets, bays, marshes and rivers. These watery locations provided pirates with a place to hide before ambushing Spanish vessels and for pirate ships to duck into and hide to avoid capture by Spanish officials. The many remote waterways, especially the thick marshes, also provided a secluded location for pirates to hide their treasure, keeping it accessible should they need to come back and retrieve it.

Additionally, the Dry Tortugas were home to a plethora of privateers, pirates, bandits, runaway slaves and angry merchants who threatened Spanish ships and plundered the coastal towns. As more Spanish settlers made their way to the New World, pirates continued to patrol the region, making Florida a profitable place to call home.

In addition to having plenty of ships, towns and people to rob, Florida's coastline was full of coral reefs and shallow areas. This caused many

Artistic drawings of ships at sea, including a shipwreck during a storm. *Library of Congress, C. Kopper.*

shipwrecks, and when the shipwrecks were abandoned, the vessels became easy pickings for pirates to collect the many treasures left behind.

Finally, many people living in communities in Florida during the early days of America lived in poverty. Because of this, when a pirate needed a place to hide or a secret to be kept, it was easy to pay people to remain quiet. Over time, pirates became folk heroes, providing more money and goods to people than their government did.

3

HOW DID PIRACY AFFECT FLORIDA?

Not only were the lives of swashbucklers changed since the settlement along Florida's coastline began, but the lives of Florida settlers were also forever changed. Spanish settlers lived in fear, waiting for the next pirate attack. This fear caused many to move farther inland, away from shores where pirates had easy access, and several packed up and relocated to other parts of the country, the Caribbean and Mexico, fleeing the wrath of angry pirates.

The presence of pirates throughout coastal areas, including the Caribbean and Gulf of Mexico, significantly affected merchant ships and passenger vessels. To avoid pirates, ship captains made travel plans far away from the waters where pirates were known to be present. The diversions taken to avoid pirates affected the number of new settlers in the region and businesses in Florida waiting for goods and materials from Spain.

It is also believed that if it were not for pirates, Britain may have struggled to hold on to the American colonies. Pirate activity in Florida attacked and negatively affected Spanish settlers, forcing Spain to give up some of its New World empires to escape the lasting effects of piracy.

Pirates influenced communities along Florida's coastline, and the presence of pirates throughout history continues to affect many people's lives today. Though there are some doubts that pirates buried their treasure in Florida, many believe that treasure awaits them, hidden deep in wetland areas. Those who believe in the legends of pirate booty buried deep in the sand have searched for the hidden chests of gold, tools and

Replica ships and participants reenact pirate battles during the Billy Bowlegs Festival in Fort Walton Beach. *State Library and Archives of Florida, Karl E. Holland.*

precious gems. These modern-day pirates and treasure hunters dedicate their lives and finances to finding these hidden treasures.

Piracy in Florida was a big deal, and the effects of historical events related to pirates occupying coastal areas continue today. This book will take you on a journey into the lives, legends and ghostly encounters of the Florida pirates, showcasing how piracy affects Florida's history and the lives of many residents today.

4
WHY ARE PIRATES HAUNTING FLORIDA?

The reasons why pirates haunt Florida are nearly endless. Likely these spirits remain behind and haunt the Sunshine State because they have unfinished business, such as still looking for their lost treasure or dealing with an enemy to seek revenge for their death or other wrongdoing.

Other theories include that the pirates like it in Florida and have chosen to remain behind in the afterlife. They may also be attached to items such as clothing, lost treasure, tools and ships.

Additionally, it is possible that the energy from when pirates ruled Florida has imprinted on the environment, which, when released, causes residual haunting activity. This theory means the energy gets trapped within the surrounding environment and replays the events like a soundtrack set on repeat. The events from the past play over and over, causing what appears to be paranormal activity, but the spirits do not interact with the living. When spirits do not react to the living, it often means it is a residual haunting repeating through time and not the actual energy or spirit of the pirate.

There are many museums throughout Florida where various pirate-related artifacts are stored. These items could not only serve as a vessel for these spirits to hang around in the present day but also act as trigger objects, encouraging pirate spirits to remain behind and interact with the living.

Similar to this theory, the many pirate-themed events—such as the Gasparilla Pirate Festival in Tampa or the Billy Bowlegs Festival in Fort Walton Beach—can trigger pirate spirits out from the shadows. Finally,

Top: Close-up view showing historical reenactment of the Ybor City invasion during the Gasparilla Carnival in Tampa, circa 1900. *State Library and Archives of Florida.*

Bottom: Costumed pirate at the helm of a ship during the Gasparilla Festival in Tampa, Florida. *State Library and Archives of Florida, Karl E. Holland.*

these reenactments could also act as a means of self-manifesting pirate spirits, almost like an egregore or thought-form. This is where the collective consciousness of many believers work together to create a supernatural entity when there was not one there.

With so many Floridians and visitors believing in pirate spirits, there is an excellent possibility that some of the paranormal activity attached to these spirits is simply a matter of self-manifestation.

Regardless of why Florida is haunted by pirate spirits, the Sunshine State is well known for some of the most famous paranormal encounters, stories, legends and spirits.

PART I

FLORIDA PIRATES

5

THE LEGEND OF BLACK CAESAR

Henri Caesar, also known as Black Caesar, is Florida's most notorious Black pirate. His story is fascinating enough to make a summer blockbuster movie.

The legend of Black Caesar is an intriguing story about the notorious pirate who made Elliott Key his home. From there, he preyed on passing ships, attacking, looting and raiding these unsuspecting vessels. He was even known for hiding on the island and other nearby places along the southeast coast of Florida while he raided local villages.

Black Caesar was an African war chieftain with immense strength and a keen intelligence. In Africa, he spent much of his time evading capture by slave traders, but one day, a dishonest slave trader tricked him into boarding a slave ship under the disguise of obtaining treasure. By the time he realized he had been deceived, the crew of the slave ship had pulled up the anchor, and the ship was far from the shoreline. This vessel was on its way to the West Indies in the hopes of making a fortune by selling their captives into slavery.

Shortly after befriending one of the white crew members, Black Caesar was able to make his escape when the ship encountered a hurricane off the Florida coast. During the chaos of this massive storm, Black Caesar and his new friend escaped in a longboat loaded with ammunition and other supplies. They were the only two known to survive the ship, and those left on board did not make it out of the storm alive.

Hailing passing vessels for help, the two men posed as shipwrecked sailors. When the ships approached and got close enough, the pair pulled out their

Portrait drawing of Blackbeard standing in front of a naval battle happening in the background. *Library of Congress.*

guns, robbing their would-be rescuers. This tactic went on for many years until the two had a falling out over a woman that ended in a duel where Black Caesar killed his longtime friend.

The deception of passing ships was just the beginning of his pirate days, which went on for many years as he continued attacking unsuspecting ships in the open sea. Legend claims he amassed a fortune in gold and gemstones and had a harem of more than one hundred women, which he hid on Elliott Key. Caesar also had a secret prison where he held men for whom he had hoped to claim ransom. Many of his prisoners perished in his jail, with most dying of starvation because Caesar did not leave enough provisions for them to survive on.

After pirating alone for many years, Caesar finally joined the crew of the notable pirate Blackbeard. While working for Blackbeard, Caesar served aboard the *Queen Anne's Revenge*. Unfortunately, his service was short-lived, because Blackbeard died in 1718 at the hands of Lieutenant Robert Maynard, leaving Caesar and a few other crewmates as the only survivors.

Then, in December 1718, Black Caesar was captured and taken to Williamsburg, Virginia, where he was tried and convicted of multiple counts of piracy. There, in Williamsburg, Caesar was hanged for his crimes, which ultimately ended this notorious pirate's life.

Though most documents claim Caesar died at the end of a hangman's noose, some reports share details about how Caesar escaped and lived out his life in hiding as authorities hanged someone else in his place, claiming it was Caesar. Another story claims Caesar was acquitted, but no specific details are available about the validity of this conspiracy theory.

Caesar was well known for terrorizing the Florida Keys before joining Blackbeard's crew. His actions as a solo pirate and aboard the *Queen Anne's Revenge* have inspired many legends and stories. Some of the legends shared about Caesar are based on his real-life adventures, while others are purely fictional accounts shared to warn villagers to beware of invading pirates.

This story about Caesar is one of the most popular ones shared, but as with many pirates who explored Florida, there are many versions of these legends. Several of these legends also claim that his treasure is buried along the Florida beaches where he once set up his residence on Elliott Key. Thousands of treasure hunters have attempted to find Caesar's treasure, but none have succeeded.

Legend claims Caesar captured and imprisoned a few children who one day escaped their jail cells. These children managed to survive on a diet of berries and shellfish and eventually started their own society. These children developed their own customs and language, creating what is often referred to as the Society of Lost Children. The idea of these children living on their own on a secluded island has raised local superstition and led to the idea that the island is haunted.

Several people have reported seeing apparitions of what they believe to be the spirits of pirates throughout Key West, on Elliott Key and in other regions where Caesar explored and pillaged. Some believe Caesar's spirit wanders the beaches of Key West at night in search of his lost treasure or as a measure to protect his treasure buried in the sand.

6
THE LEGEND OF JOSÉ GASPAR

José Gaspar, Florida's infamous Spanish pirate known as Gasparilla, was believed to have lived from 1756 until 1821. During his reign of piracy, Gaspar terrorized communities along the Gulf of Mexico and vessels that dared to enter the waters he patrolled. He rose to pirate royalty during Florida's second Spanish period from 1783 to 1821, but not all believe the legends behind Gasparilla are true, and some believe he never existed.

There are minimal details about Gaspar's life and very little about his early life, motivation and piratical adventures and exploits. Additionally, while many agree that he was an active buccaneer, many legends about Gasparilla differ tremendously. With many legends surrounding Gaspar's life, most stories share similarities, including that he was a very wealthy pirate, amassing much of his fortune by stealing and ransoming the hostages he captured during his long piracy career.

Though many stories and legends about Gaspar make him a popular figure in Florida folklore, there is no physical evidence he existed. Several legends also claim that Gaspar died when he leaped from his ship to avoid being captured by the U.S. Navy. Upon his death, he left behind a hidden treasure, which, if true, has yet to be discovered.

Throughout documented history, Gaspar's life, exploits and presence are not mentioned in Spanish or American court records, ship logs, newspapers or other written archives. Additionally, no physical artifacts connected to Gaspar have been discovered, especially in southwest Florida, known as his "pirate kingdom."

Many researchers agree that Gaspar was a pirate born around 1756 in Spain. He served in the Spanish navy prior to becoming a pirate around 1783. Another fact most agree on is that he died in southwest Florida during a battle against the U.S. Navy in late 1821. However, though these facts are similar, several retellings of his life story differ. The differences could be an indication that José Gaspar never truly existed.

While no historical documents mention Gaspar, there is a written mention of him in a short biography in a 1900s promotional brochure for the Gasparilla Inn. Set on Gasparilla Island at Charlotte Harbor, the inn created a legend to draw the interest of travelers looking for a pirate-themed adventure.

The brochure's author freely admitted it was a dramatic tale he created as a work of fiction "without a true fact in it."[1]

Later, the details of the Gaspar legend were embellished, creating a legend based on the fanciful account of an early marketing campaign. The legend of José Gaspar was included in a 1923 book about real pirates, which added to the confusion surrounding Gasparilla's life and his legend as Florida's most infamous Spanish pirate.[2]

The truth behind Gaspar's nonexistence did not stop the spread of his legend; throughout the years, many new versions of his life story started to emerge. Some stories claim he began his life as a poverty-stricken Spanish youth desperate for money. He kidnapped a young girl for ransom. When he was arrested for the kidnapping, he was given a choice—join the navy or spend time in prison. He chose to join the navy, where he served with distinction before leading a mutiny against the ship's tyrannical captain. When the mutiny ended, he fled to Florida with his newly stolen ship.

Other tales related to Gaspar's life include being a nobleman who achieved a high rank in the Spanish Royal Navy and was wanted in Spain for stealing the crown jewels. One story claims he stole the crown jewels, while others claim a jilted lover falsely accused him.

No matter what story about Gaspar's origins is told, his life as a pirate began because he wanted to seek revenge against Spain for his treatment as a young man. His rampage as a pirate took him around the world, leading him to settle in an uninhabited area along the southwest coast of Spanish Florida around 1783. His ship, the *Floriblanca*,[3] had a home base on what is known today as Gasparilla Island.

To add to the mystery and legend behind Gasparilla, a mysterious box was found by a local construction worker in the 1930s. Ernesto Lopez claimed he found the box while working with a repair crew servicing the Cass Street

Bridge in downtown Tampa.[4] According to the stories, the mysterious wooden box contained a pile of Spanish and Portuguese coins, a treasure map and a severed hand wearing a ring with an engraving—"Gaspar."[5]

Lopez believed he had discovered Gaspar's hand with his treasure map indicating where he buried his famous cache near the Hillsborough River in Tampa. He hid the box in the attic to be rediscovered by his great-grandchildren in 2015, and they had the contents of the wooden box examined by the Tampa Bay History Center. The box contained nonprecious coins, a plat map from the 1920s and souvenirs from early Gasparilla Festivals and parades. The origin of the hand remains a mystery, but the curator of the history center believed it might be a mummified monkey hand.[6]

To help Gaspar's legend live on, Tampa celebrates the life of this fictional pirate annually during its Gasparilla Pirate Festival. This festival occurs throughout Tampa and features a large parade, community events and more. Since 1904, this festival has celebrated the life and crew of the mythical pirate, including the *Jose Gasparilla II*, a 165-foot-long pirate ship complete with a swashbuckling crew. More than 300,000 people attend the Gasparilla Festival annually, providing the community more than $20 million in local revenue.

Some people have reported seeing Gaspar's apparition walking along the shores of Gasparilla Island and near the Boca Grande Lighthouse. But if he is a fictional character, could his spiritual appearance be an egregore or thought form? Or is the appearance of his spirit proof that the legend of José Gaspar was real? Either way, his life and hauntings remain a mystery.

Some believe he is searching for his buried treasure, while others think he may seek revenge against those who did him wrong. It is also possible he continues to search for his lost love, whom he buried headless on the shores of Gasparilla Island.

Many businesses in Florida have taken advantage of Gaspar's name, using his name for their business and events. This photo shows a local Flagler Beach store—Jose Gaspar Treasure Co. *State Library and Archives of Florida.*

One of the most commonly shared love stories associated with Gaspar's legend and ghostly visitations is that of "Gasparilla's Headless Princess." This story is full of mystery, superstition and the supernatural, as it claims the infamous pirate could be hanging around the area in spirit form as punishment for his heinous crimes, including the kidnapping of a Spanish princess. Some people have seen the apparition of a headless woman roaming the beaches near the Boca Grande Lighthouse, which is believed to be the princess's spirit.

According to legend, Gaspar was collecting beautiful women, many of whom he held captive on Captiva Island. One of his captives, Josefa, a Spanish princess, caught Gaspar's eye, and he wanted to have her as his own. However, Josefa wanted nothing to do with Gaspar, and the more he tried to gain her admiration, the further she pulled away from him.

One day, she was so upset and agitated with his consistent romantic gestures she spat in his face in the hopes to get him to leave her alone. However, that did not work in her favor. Gaspar pulled his sword out and, in a fit of rage, cut Josefa's head off.

Distraught over killing the woman he loved, Gaspar took her body to his island, where he buried it. Legend claims he buried only her body, and there are no indications of what he did with her head, leading many to believe he kept the head with him until he died in the 1820s.

To this day, people have reported seeing a headless spirit, believed to belong to the Spanish princess, on the shores of Gasparilla Island. Several believe she continues her search in the afterlife, looking for her missing head. Gaspar has also made his presence known at Gasparilla Island State Park, where witnesses have seen him scouring the shoreline, searching for his buried treasure.

Other sightings of Gaspar include several guests seeing his apparition roaming the Tortuga Inn Beach Resort halls in Bradenton Beach. Some visitors have come face-to-face with the apparition, and others have heard disembodied voices and experienced strange occurrences they claim were caused by this notorious pirate.

At this point in time, the question of whether the infamous pirate José Gaspar was real or fictional is irrelevant. Today, his legend lives on, and that's what leads many people to visit the southwest regions of Florida in search of his lost pirate treasure or for an opportunity to run into his spirit. He may even make an appearance in the crowds watching the festivities of the Gasparilla Festival and no one even know he is there.

7

THE LEGEND OF ROBERT SEARLE

R obert Searle was an English pirate best known for the destruction he caused throughout the St. Augustine area. Searle's mission as a pirate was to search for the silver ingots housed in the royal treasurer's stores. He and his crew sailed from Jamaica, heading for St. Augustine on a Spanish vessel they captured while in Havana.

With the help of his crew, he captured the ship off the coast of Cuba and used it to sneak into St. Augustine's harbor. One of the men aboard the ship captured by Searle previously resided in St. Augustine, and he was willing to help Searle and his crew navigate the inlet in preparation for the attack on the town.

As a former resident of St. Augustine, Pedro Piques was run out of town by the governor, leaving him with anger toward his former hometown. Without hesitation, he helped the pirate crew navigate the inlet. Upon docking, Searle and his crew patiently waited until midnight, when they began attacking the city.

As Searle and his men attacked the city, residents ran out of their homes into the city streets to see what all the commotion was about. Being in the streets made them easy targets, and many were killed or captured, while only a few made it safely into nearby woods, where they sought safety until the end of the raid.

During the raid, Searle and his crew raided local businesses, homes, government buildings and the community church. Though 120 Spanish soldiers were stationed in St. Augustine in May 1668 at the time of the horrific attack, they were unable to defend the city and its residents. The night of the attack, a fisherman rowed ashore screaming at the soldiers that he had been attacked and shot by pirates, and moments after hearing the man's screams, the town was under siege. Searle's entire crew started rampaging around St. Augustine.

Searle's crew killed more than sixty St. Augustine citizens during the attack, which at the time was approximately one-quarter of the city's population. In addition to those who lost their lives, several residents were captured and held hostage with a high ransom demand. All hostages were released after the pirates received food, weapons, gold, silver and other supplies in exchange for release. Non-white residents, including Native Americans and enslaved Africans, were sent off to be sold into slavery in the labor-hungry Caribbean.

After Searle attacked St. Augustine, as he and his men were leaving, he vowed he would return one day to take complete control of the city. Searle's men did not destroy the entire town of St. Augustine; however, after the attack, many throughout the area remained on high alert and became

St. George Street in St. Augustine. *Library of Congress.*

Fort Marion, before being renamed Castillo de San Marcos, sits and protects St. Augustine residents. *Library of Congress.*

suspicious of strangers for fear the pirates would return for a second attack on the town. Undoubtedly, Searle's attack on St. Augustine created a lasting imprint on the area, which could cause many of the paranormal events reported throughout America's oldest town.

The Spanish queen regent Mariana was determined never to let an attack like this happen again because St. Augustine played a pivotal role in shipping supplies between Cuba, Florida and Spain. The Spanish dedicated any available funds toward defending Florida's coastline and built a massive coquina fort. With the construction of Fort Marion, later renamed Castillo de San Marcos, complete, St. Augustine never fell victim to another pirate attack. The citizens were prepared to defeat offensive attacks on the city.

Searle continued his piracy, teaming up with other legendary pirates, including Sir Henry Morgan, when living in Central America. In 1674, shortly after he relocated to Honduras, Searle was killed in a duel with an Indigenous logwood cutter.

During the attack on St. Augustine, Searle left many dead, including several small children. A five-year-old girl died at the hands of Searle during his murderous rampage on the town. Legends claim that the young girl's spirit attached herself to Searle, haunting him for many years. Many believe her spirit made him mad, causing him to lose focus and appear erratic.

8

THE LEGEND OF
SIR FRANCIS DRAKE

About eighty years before Robert Searle attacked St. Augustine, Sir Francis Drake left his mark on the city. Born around 1542 in Tavistock, United Kingdom, Drake was the eldest of twelve sons. At the age of twelve, he became an apprentice on a ship and worked through the ranks of the English military until he was knighted in 1581 and earned the rank of vice admiral in 1588 during the fight against the Spanish Armada.

Drake's early career at sea started when he was placed in the household of sea captain William Hawkins of Plymouth, a relative. During his time with Hawkins, he worked as an apprentice on many of Hawkins's boats. He became a purser by the age of eighteen and later worked to help small traders between the Medway River and the Dutch coast. Additionally, some anecdotal evidence claims that Drake served as an ordinary seaman on at least two of Sir John Hawkins's slaving voyages.

Drake was a soldier, privateer and explorer who played a significant role in Florida's history, especially in the 1500s, when England was starting to claim more land in America. Because of his success during the raids of Panama in 1572 and 1573, he was sent from England to attack Spanish settlements in 1585.

Drake was a privateer and explorer for England, but the Spanish feared him, branding him as a pirate. His vicious attacks and numerous successful raids against Spanish ships and settlements earned Drake the nickname "El Draque" or the Dragon. Many Spanish mariners feared him because several stories and legends were shared throughout Spanish

Portrait of Sir Francis Drake. *Library of Congress.*

Replica of *Revenge*, a ship Sir Francis Drake commanded many times between the years 1587 and 1589. *Library of Congress.*

settlements and among Spanish soldiers that Drake was believed to have practiced witchcraft.

Though Drake was known worldwide for his horrific attacks on Spanish vessels and settlements, he was best known for his explorations, including his circumnavigation of the world. In a single expedition, Drake and his crew completed the first English circumnavigation of the world between 1577 and 1580, and it was the third circumnavigation overall.

After Drake returned to England, Hawkins accused Drake of desertion. Additionally, Drake was accused of stealing the treasure they accumulated when he distributed all the profits among the crew. These accusations and the fallout with Hawkins led Drake to pursue other ventures. He dedicated his life to attacking Spanish possessions wherever he could. Throughout his career at sea, Drake continued exploration efforts and attacked Spanish vessels and communities.

Drake's at-sea adventures led him on a great expedition to America, which Queen Elizabeth I ordered as a preemptive strike against Spain. Drake was ordered to attack the Spanish colonies after signing the Treaty of Nonsuch in September 1585. Drake was in command of twenty-one ships carrying 1,800 soldiers under Christopher Carleill.

The first stop along Drake's expedition was Vigo, Spain, where they attacked the city and held their ground for two weeks while ransoming supplies. Drake and his crew also plundered Santiago in the Cape Verde Islands, attacked the port of Santo Domingo and captured the city of Cartagena de Indias in present-day Colombia. In Cartagena, he assisted in releasing one hundred enslaved Turks before returning to his voyage on June 6, 1586.

Drake finally reached his final destination, attacking a wooden Spanish fort at San Agustin (St. Augustine) in Spanish Florida. The small fort was set in the sand dunes, and the Spanish soldiers fired only a few shots before fleeing the area. Drake sent a landing party led by Christopher Carleill, captain of the *Tiger*, who rowed a boat into the inlet looking for signs of Spaniards. No Spaniards were spotted, and the landing party encountered a French Huguenot, Nicholas Borgoignon, who had been captured by the Spanish six years before. Borgoignon agreed to help Drake's landing party, guiding them to the Spanish settlement.

At the start of the attack, St. Augustine's Spanish governor, Pedro Menéndez de Márquez, received a warning Drake was off the coast. Upon realizing there were fewer than one hundred militiamen, he found providing any successful form of resistance nearly impossible. In response, the Spanish settlers withdrew inland away from the town, hoping to make a surprise raid against the English later. During the day, Drake and his men occupied the wooden fort, but at night, Native Americans, who were allies of the Spanish garrison, went into town and attacked the English invaders.

The first attack on the English lasted about twenty minutes, during which time the Native Americans realized they were losing and retreated into nearby wooded areas. The next day, Drake, Carleill and about two hundred men made their way up the inlet in small boats to a Spanish log stockade fort. With few losses, the English landed and took control of the fort as the Spanish fled farther inland.

Upon further inspection of the fort, the English found an intact gun platform with fourteen bronze artillery pieces, a chest containing the garrison's pay and many other items they were able to plunder. When they were done, Drake and his crew burned the fort to the ground.

After leaving the log stockade fort, Drake and his crew found the main settlement of St. Augustine without anyone anywhere in the town. The English found some Spanish soldiers outside the city, and the two opened a skirmishing fire. Carleill's men charged toward the outskirts of town into the scrub, forcing the Spaniards to retreat. This charge left Drake in control of the St. Augustine settlement.

That night, the English collected everything they could from the town and, the following day, razed the entire St. Augustine settlement to the ground. Drake's men torched buildings and destroyed crops, artillery pieces were carried away and anything of value was taken by pirates.

By the end of the attack, the town had burned to the ground, and Drake sailed for Roanoake, where Sir Walter Raleigh had established a new settlement.

During a sea voyage to Panama, Drake died from dysentery on January 28, 1596. He was buried in a lead coffin, dressed in his full suit of armor and buried at sea off the coast of Portobelo. Many divers have attempted to locate Drake's lead coffin, but to this day, his body remains lost at sea.

St. Augustine is one of the most haunted cities in America, and many believe the spirits still roaming are from when Drake commanded the English rampage against the Spanish. Visitors and residents claim to experience odd occurrences throughout town, especially in areas where the English raid occurred—everything from hearing disembodied voices and bloodcurdling cries to gun and cannon fire and seeing apparitions in period Spanish and English military attire.

There is no doubt St. Augustine is haunted. Though some want to believe the spirits are from this time in Florida's history, including encountering the spirit of Drake, it is challenging to determine who haunts the area. Chances are that some spirits are from when Drake and his men raided St. Augustine, but there is also a chance that the spirits could be from a different time.

9
THE LEGEND OF ANDREW RANSON

Throughout early Florida history, St. Augustine was one of the most targeted cities in America, continually fighting off attacks from invading forces, such as pirates. Though notorious pirates such as Drake and Searle rampaged the area, residents feared the team of Captain Thomas Jingle and his trusted ship steward Andrew Ranson.

Around 1684, Ranson had a large following of men who served Captain Jingle in a large fleet from the Bahamas to St. Augustine. Ranson's men were loyal to him, and since Ranson was loyal to Jingle, they were also faithful to the pirate captain. Jingle dreamed of the riches St. Augustine was rumored to house and developed an elaborate plan to raid the city, promising all those who joined him a hefty payout.

Unfortunately, a massive storm came out of nowhere before landfall, sinking most of the ships in Jingle's fleet. Jingle and Ranson survived, and along with a crew of six men, Ranson was sent ashore by Jingle to a section of land north of St. Augustine. While there, Ranson stocked up on supplies with the intention of the crew returning to the Bahamas to regroup.

However, the area was heavily surveilled by Spanish sentinels lurking around every corner. The sentinels were tasked with waiting for pirates to enter the area and strike in an effort to force them out and thwart any potential threats of attack. During their trip ashore to gather supplies, Ranson and his men were captured and brought to St. Augustine, where they were imprisoned.

Upon entering the city limits, Governor Juan Marques Cabrera tortured all of the captured men in an attempt to obtain information about Jingle's plans. Holding onto their loyalty to Captain Jingle, neither Ranson nor his men revealed any info about Jingle's plans.

Frustrated and furious, Cabrera sentenced Ranson to be executed using one of the most gruesome deaths suffered by a pirate—death by garrote. This form of execution uses a garrote, a special noose that uses a twisting handle to increase tension around the neck. It was a slow and painful strangulation that only ended with death.

With his back to the garrote pole, Ranson stood with shaking hands, clutching a rosary as the noose was placed around his neck. The executioner twisted the garrote six times, and even though Ranson's body had gone limp, he tightened it one more time to ensure Ranson was dead. However, during the seventh twist of the garrote, the rope snapped, releasing Ranson's body, which fell to the ground in a heap.

Father Perez de la Mota rushed toward the fallen pirate to prepare him for eternal rest. Upon getting to Ranson's body, the city priest realized he was still breathing, which was unheard of after suffering the wrath of the garrote. Father Perez believed this to be a sign from God, indicating that Ranson was meant to live, and he brought the pirate back to the church's sanctuary.

The governor was livid and fought for the priest to allow him to execute Ranson, but Father Perez refused to hand the pirate over to authorities. The priest continued to protect Ranson until Cabrera was called back to Spain and was succeeded by Governor Don Diego Losada. Eventually, Lasoda and Father Perez made a deal granting Ranson amnesty as long as the condemned pirate assist in the construction of Castillo de San Marcos.

Ranson agreed to the terms and was finally granted his freedom in 1702 after assisting in St. Augustine's defense against an English invasion.

Today, stories about Ranson's life as a pirate have been told and retold in books, articles, movies and television shows. Many of these stories consider him to be the most famous pirate to have lived in St. Augustine. Though other pirates came before and after him, he was most famous for the legendary story in which he was able to escape death and was saved in those final moments.

Several people believe Ranson's spirit haunts St. Augustine. Visitors and locals have reported seeing an apparition in pirate attire walking the streets and alleyways near Castillo de San Marcos. One visitor captured a photo that appeared on the Travel Channel's *Ghost Adventures*, believed to have captured the spirit of Ranson when no one else was in the area dressed like the ghostly image captured in the photograph.

Could Ranson's spirit be roaming St. Augustine? Anything is possible, especially since this was the location where he was sentenced to death. Luck intervened, saving his life and causing a psychic imprint and possible spiritual connection between Ranson and the St. Augustine area.

10

MORE LEGENDS OF NOTORIOUS FLORIDA PIRATES

There is no denying Florida was tragically affected during the Golden Era of Piracy. Many pirates came and went throughout those years, leaving a path of destruction behind them. Some pirates, like Black Caesar and Andrew Ranson, spent many years living in Florida; others made only brief appearances in the Sunshine State. Some of these brief appearances resulted in a long-lasting imprint, causing paranormal activity throughout the state. In contrast, others have left no identifiable hauntings behind; there is still a strong possibility that some of the following pirates live on as spirits in Florida.

HENRY JENNINGS

Henry Jennings heard rumors that a fleet of ships carried valuable Spanish treasures from Cuba; however, these ships never reached their destination. In 1715, the Spanish treasure ships became trapped within a hurricane near Port St. Lucie, leading to the ships crashing and dispersing valuable jewels, gold and silver throughout the shallow waters in the area up to Melbourne Beach.

When Jennings and his crew arrived in Florida, they discovered several survivors of the shipwrecks attempting to collect and save as much treasure as possible. Leading an attack on the survivors, Jennings captured a significant amount of the Spanish treasure. Jennings and his crew managed to steal more than 340,000 pieces of eight from the storehouse holding the gathered treasure, and during the attack, they killed one person.

Jennings then returned a second time, sealing more treasure. After the second attack, Jennings retired from piracy and lived a wealthy life until his death in 1745.

Jennings's attack on the Spanish survivors and other notorious pirates emerging to popularity during the Golden Age of Piracy led the English government to take action against pirates in the Caribbean and issue a royal proclamation in 1717. The English government would seek out, convict and execute anyone caught conducting acts of piracy. However, those who signed the proclamation were pardoned and forced to retire.

BLACKBEARD

Blackbeard, also known as Edward Teach and Edward Thatch, was a notorious pirate known and feared throughout the Caribbean and West Indies. After serving as a sailor on privateer ships during Queen Anne's War, he turned to a life of piracy.

He sailed a fleet of pirate ships responsible for terrorizing and wreaking havoc up and down Florida's east coast. Several pirates, including Black Caesar and Henry Jennings, encountered and partnered with Blackbeard at one point during their piracy careers.

Before leaving Florida waters, Blackbeard went to the Melbourne Beach area, where he also took advantage of the wrecked 1715 Spanish Fleet.

Under the Royal Act of Grace, Blackbeard accepted a pardon and retired happily, enjoying his massive loot until he died on November 22, 1718.

FRANCISCO MENENDEZ

Born in The Gambia of West Africa, Francisco Menendez was brought to Southern Carolina as an enslaved person. He managed to escape to Florida in 1724 and assisted in the construction of Fort Mose, north of St. Augustine. He served the Spanish Empire as a Black militiaman, leading the construction efforts for the new fort. During his leadership of the fort's construction, Menendez was joined by forty formerly enslaved people who came to settle outside the fort and create the first free and legal African American community in North America.

After developing and leading the community, Menendez set his sights on the seas aboard a Spanish ship he used to raid unsuspecting English vessels entering Caribbean and Florida waters.

CALICO JACK

Englishman John Rackham, also known as Calico Jack, was a flamboyant pirate known for acts of piracy throughout the Bahamas, Cuba and Florida. His piracy career occurred close to the end of the Golden Age of Piracy, and he is most remembered for having two female crew members—Mary Read and his wife, Anne Bonny.

Calico Jack received a king's pardon in 1719 but returned to piracy after meeting Bonny, who was married then. The two cooperated by stealing a British sloop in 1720 when Bonny joined him and his crew. Eventually, he was captured by Jonathan Barnet; put on trial by the governor of Jamaica, Nicolas Lawes; and hanged in November 1720.

ANNE BONNY

Irish pirate Anne Bonny was married to James Bonny when she met Calico Jack. As one of the few female pirates in recorded history, Bonny mainly operated in the Caribbean, often making her appearance known along the east coast of Florida.

Very little is known about Bonny's life, but there are reports that she met and married Calico Jack. She was captured along with her husband in 1720 and was sentenced to death, but her execution was stayed because she was pregnant.

MARY READ

Mary Read, also known as Mark Read, was an English pirate who initially disguised her identity by representing herself as a man. She and Anne Bonny served during the Golden Age of Piracy as part of Calico Jack's crew.

Read, along with Calico Jack and Bonny, were captured, convicted of acts of piracy and sentenced to hang. However, Read and Bonny escaped the hangman's noose because the two claimed to be pregnant. Their executions were delayed. Bonny's fate after the trial is unknown, and Read died in prison in April 1721.

LUIS-MICHEL AURY

Luis-Michel Aury, a French privateer, was best known for occupying Amelia Island and conducting acts of piracy throughout the Caribbean and Gulf of Mexico. In 1817, Aury was forced out of Florida after President James Monroe intervened to oust Aury's fleet of pirates. When his fleet left Florida, it was the last significantly sized pirate fleet to leave the Sunshine State.

Though no official records recognize Aury as assisting any of the countries he served, he was considered a member of the Great Colombia Liberation Fighters. This affiliation was determined because of his close affiliation with Simón Bolívar.

CAPTAIN KIDD

Captain Kidd is best known for legends associated with leaving pots of money in holes in the ground from Key West, Florida, to Halifax, Nova Scotia. The money believed to be buried along North America's East Coast was from his reckless adventures, where he collected a massive amount of riches, including doubloons and guineas.

Kidd was best known for a sea superstition: his ship was often confused with the *Flying Dutchman*, which was usually seen as an apparition before disappearing into the horizon.

CHARLES VANE

English pirate Charles Vane mainly operated in the Bahamas during the Golden Age of Piracy. Still, when the 1715 Spanish Treasure Fleet wrecked off the coast of Florida, he made his way to the area in an attempt to collect some of the lost treasure under the leadership of Henry Jennings.

Vane was a cruel pirate known for beating, torturing and killing captured sailors. He continued his rampage until he was discovered by a passing British ship after being caught in a storm. He was arrested and tried in Port Royal, where he was found guilty and hanged in March 1721.

HENRY EVERY

Henry Every, also known as Henry Avery, was an English pirate best known for wreaking havoc throughout Florida waters. Every had many aliases, including Benjamin Bridgeman and Long Ben, and contemporaries dubbed him "The Arch Pirate" and "The King of Pirates."

Every's legend is unique from other pirates because he managed to be one of the few prominent pirate captains to escape with all of his treasure without being killed in battle or arrested. Though his career was short, lasting only two years, his exploits gained the public's attention, inspiring works of literature. Several pirates claim they were inspired to hit the open seas as pirates thanks to Every's legend.

CAPTAIN HENRY MORGAN

Captain Morgan, also known as Sir Henry Morgan and Harri Morgan, was a Welsh pirate and plantation owner. Much of his early life is unknown, including how he ended up in the Caribbean or how he came to serve as lieutenant governor of Jamaica.

From his home base in Port Royal, he raided settlements and shipping vessels on the Spanish Main. He became very wealthy doing this through the Caribbean and Florida waters, took the money he looted and purchased three large sugar plantations in Jamaica. Morgan's pirate life inspired many pirate-themed works of fiction, including retellings his stories in literature, poetry and film.

HENRY ROSS

Henry Ross is believed to have served as captain under Jean Lafitte, and Ross Island was his base of operation. It is rumored he buried his treasure on the one-mile-long (north to south) and one-half-mile-wide island. Set in the Upper Tampa Bay area near St. Petersburg, Ross Island, named after nineteenth-century inhabitant Lorenzo Ross, holds the secret of Henry Ross's lost treasure.

Ross Island became a lair for pirates looking for a place to hide as they preyed on merchant ships entering and docking in the Tampa Bay area. The island became a pirate colony, and Henry Ross was its ruler. He first buried his chest of gold around 1821 and continued to bury more treasure. The location of his treasure was lost, and many still believe that several of his treasure chests remain buried under the island's surface.

HENRY CASTOR

English pirate Henry Castor is little known, but it is believed he sailed throughout the Gulf of Mexico in the mid-1700s. Egmont Key, formerly Castor Key, is rumored to have been where he buried much of his treasure. Castor would appear occasionally, seeking out treasure and terrorizing beachside communities of Florida's west coast.

PART II
CITIES HAUNTED BY PIRATES

11

THE LOST LIGHTHOUSE OF SULPHUR SPRINGS

Sulphur Springs, part of the Tampa area, is no stranger to paranormal activity and filled with pockets of historical interest where the past continues to live in the present. This area of Florida is known for many mysterious happenings, unexpected ghostly encounters and eerie sights. Many of these paranormal experiences seem to occur near a water tower that stands where a lighthouse once stood, guiding pirates along the Gulf coastline.

The quiet area of Sulphur Springs is about five miles north of downtown Tampa and has been a serene place for people to visit and experience the mineral springs' benefits since the late 1800s. Today, the towering water tower can be seen from Florida's Interstate 275 and serves as a reminder of the many tragic events in the area.

A lighthouse once stood where the Sulphur Springs Water Tower sits today. It guided pirates and ship captains along the Gulf Coast and served as a watchtower for invading ships entering the Tampa Bay area. The lighthouse was torn down many years later, leaving a dark spot on Tampa's coastline.

The area was used as a major tourist attraction throughout the years following the destruction of the lighthouse. But Josiah Richardson, the great mind behind this endeavor, experienced many tragedies, never bringing his entire dream to life. He opened Mave's Arcade, Florida's first indoor shopping venue, on the first floor of his Sulphur Springs Hotel and Apartments.

He realized he needed better water pressure for his guests and residents, so he built a water tower nearby. Richardson had to mortgage his resort to fund the construction of the 200,000-gallon water tower.

The Sulphur Springs Hotel sits near where the lighthouse once stood. *Library of Congress.*

Unfortunately, Richardson's dream of a luxurious resort was short-lived. In 1933, the area was flooded when the Tampa Electric Company's Dam was intentionally destroyed. The Sulphur Springs Hotel and Apartments were so severely damaged that Richardson ended up bankrupt and left his dream resort behind.

Though Richardson's dream was not a reality, the area remained popular with tourists. The rumors and legends are the biggest lure to the area. The location is haunted by some of the most infamous pirates known to frequent the Gulf waters.

It is believed that since the location where the water tower stands today was once a lighthouse, it is possible pirates could have used the lighthouse as a landmark on a buried treasure map. Without the history and the guiding light from the lighthouse, the spirits of these pirates may be lost when searching for their booty in the afterlife. Ghostly images of pirates have been spotted wandering around the park that now lies under the tower as if they are searching for clues to where their hidden treasure is buried.

A ghost ship proudly flying a pirate flag has also been seen aimlessly sailing around the river as if on a quest. As the ship approaches land, it fades away until it vanishes into thin air.

With so many eyewitness accounts of pirates and the vanishing pirate ship, it is safe to say Sulphur Springs is haunted by long-dead pirates who continue to search for a treasure that has never been found.

12

JOHN'S PASS VILLAGE

MADEIRA BEACH, FLORIDA

John's Pass is a small fishing village and popular tourist destination for visitors wanting to explore local waterways, experience local cuisine and spend the day in the Florida sunshine. The community was named after John Levique, a gentleman from France who worked as a young lad on a Spanish vessel until it was attacked by pirates.

Around 1836, Levique, a French peasant, was a cabin boy on a Spanish sailing vessel. One day, the Spanish vessel was attacked by pirates, and the young Levique was given a choice—death or joining the pirate crew. He chose to join the pirates, quickly working his way through the ranks to eventually captain his ship.

Levique was different from most pirates. He did not believe in killing those he captured or holding them for ransom. Local legend claims he was a gentleman's pirate. Though he did not amass a vast fortune like many of his pirate counterparts, it is rumored that he did manage to collect enough riches to fill a small chest and bury it on an island off Florida's west coast.

He then staked land nearby in the John's Pass area, where he could keep an eye on his treasure while working as a simple turtle farmer. Unfortunately for Levique, a hurricane hit the area and altered the Pass between Treasure Island and Madeira Beach, making it impossible for Levique to find his buried treasure. Levique remained in the area until he died in 1873.

Locals living on Treasure Island and Madeira Beach have reported seeing Levique's spirit walking along the beach, searching for his lost treasure.

Below: A tour boat designed to resemble a pirate ship takes visitors on a guided tour of John's Pass and surrounding areas. *Heather Leigh, PhD.*

Right: A view of John's Pass Boardwalk where there have been several encounters with the spirits of pirates. *Heather Leigh, PhD.*

Opposite, top: John's Pass Village is a small village known for pirate-themed businesses and hauntings. *Heather Leigh, PhD.*

Opposite, bottom: As seen through palm trees, Delosa's Pizza is the location of phantom pirate footsteps. *Heather Leigh, PhD.*

Some have even claimed to have seen an apparition in pirate attire walking near the John's Pass Boardwalk late at night.

Another pirate haunting John's Pass can be found at Delosa's Pizza, which was once the location of Shanty Hogan Saloon. The saloon was where many dubious acts occurred, and it had a reputation for catering to pirates. Shanty Hogan Saloon also had a den of ill repute upstairs, but a fire destroyed the second floor.

Today, employees and patrons of Delosa's Pizza hear recurrent footsteps from what used to be the second floor. What is interesting about these footsteps is they have a unique pattern. When the footsteps begin, they sound like a stomp-click pattern, similar to the footsteps of a peg-legged man.

Famous pirates and pirate legends settled John's Pass, and many other supernatural events occur daily. There is no doubt that pirates are lingering in the shadows and searching the shores for buried treasure that has yet to be discovered.

13

CEDAR KEY

Cedar Key is home to many paranormal stories. As a popular place for pirates to bury their booty, it is not a mystery why they choose to haunt the island in the afterlife. The island off the shores of Tampa Bay is home to mysterious legends, including several notorious pirates who once pillaged and looted the area.

One unique story is about a ghost dog believed to belong to a young Annie Simpson. The dog's apparition is spotted near Shell Mount, where the Suwannee River empties into the Gulf of Mexico. No one knows what happened to Simpson or her giant wolfhound, but one day, they went out exploring and picking wildflowers and were never seen or heard from again. Legend claims that Simpson stumbled upon a buried treasure, and the

Bird's-eye view of Cedar-Key, Florida. *Library of Congress, JJ Stoner and Beck & Pauli.*

pirates to whom the treasure belonged killed her and her wolfhound to keep her quiet.

Fishermen throughout the years have reported seeing an apparition of a beautiful young girl—believed to be Simpson—wearing a blue blouse and long dark skirt standing by the edge of the wooded area of the island. Many reports claim she extends her arm and waves her hand, almost as if trying to get the fishermen to follow her deeper into the woods.

Some locals have also reported seeing the apparition of Simpson. Still, the wolfhound is what most people report seeing and encountering when walking along the beaches near where they were killed. Several paranormal encounters with Simpson and her dog end with the two of them fading into a white mist and floating over the water.

A strange discovery was made on the island. A skeleton of a large dog was discovered, but no sign of Simpson's body or skeleton was ever found. Many believe her spirit remains behind, wandering the woods, waiting for someone to find her body and bring her back home.

Throughout the years, treasure hunters have searched the area, unearthing small caches of coins. Someone claimed bits and pieces of an old iron-bound wood chest were dug up from beneath a giant oak on the island. These discoveries could possibly be the remains of pirate treasure that was once buried in Cedar Key in hopes of keeping it safe.

Though this is the only pirate-related haunting in Cedar Key, it is one unique experience, as not many people encounter the spirits of animals. So, if you dare to see if you can brave the possibility of encountering the spirit of a wolfhound, you must take the time to visit Cedar Key, Florida.

14

SEAHORSE KEY

Many Floridians grew up hearing urban legends about the numerous small islands offshore in the Gulf and along the Atlantic. Seahorse Key, part of the Cedar Keys, is one of those islands famously known for the ghost of the headless pirate known to ride a palomino at night along the beach. This mysterious apparition, described as very frightening, is believed to be Pierre LeBlanc.

Legend claims that LeBlanc was working for the notorious Jean Lafitte when he was abandoned on Seahorse Key with some supplies and a palomino. LeBlanc's duties were to guard Lafitte's treasure, which was hidden on the island. LeBlanc was to guard the entire island to protect the treasure and prevent other pirates from stumbling upon the booty.

One day, a stranger arrived at Seahorse Key and took time to befriend LeBlanc, who grew to trust the stranger fully. During a drunken night, LeBlanc passed out, and the stranger made his way to the loot. But before the would-be thief could leave the island, LeBlanc awoke and attacked the stranger. However, in the end, LeBlanc lost his head, and the stranger escaped with Lafitte's treasure.

Though this story is believed to be nothing more than a myth, many people visiting Seahorse Key report seeing the apparition of a headless man riding a palomino along the beaches of the island. As the person and the horse ride off, they slowly fade away.

One fisherman had an eerie encounter with this apparition, claiming it emerged from the sand. One day, he was lying on the beach and saw what he thought were crab claws coming up from the sand. As he looked closer, he saw fingernails and hands clawing their way up from the sand.

He remained frozen where he lay on the beach and described the hands as long and pointy, covered in black from decay. Almost as if it were in slow motion, the fisherman watched a body emerge from the sand, first the forearms, then the biceps and then the shoulders. He described it as a horrific view as the spirit looked ghost-white with severed arteries and tissue in the shoulders but no head.

West end of Seahorse Key—Levy County, Florida. *State Library and Archives of Florida.*

The fisherman finally started to move away in panic but kept stumbling as the headless man continued to emerge from the sand. When the headless man was free of the stand and approached the fisherman, the frightened beachgoer struck the sand-covered apparition before running to his boat. He called the police, and when they arrived, there was no body or remnants of a body anywhere on the island.

There is no proof that the fisherman's story is true, but it fits with the many sightings of the headless pirate and his palomino on Seahorse Key.

15

ST. AUGUSTINE

St. Augustine is a paranormal hot spot, and many investigators make their way to this part of Florida like a pack of wolves in the hopes of capturing evidence of ghosts. Many who have investigated St. Augustine encountered spirits of pirates and those associated with the massive amounts of pirate activity known in this part of the Sunshine State. Along with the many ghostly encounters, legends of pirate treasure, attack and the swashbuckling lifestyle have been shared for generations in the nation's oldest city.

Regarding Florida lore and legend, there is no more notorious English pirate than Sir Francis Drake, who was known for his exceptional navigational skills, which helped him sail around the world. Drake stopped by a small outpost in Florida on what is known today as Anastasia Island on his return trip to England using the Gulfstream current in June 1586.

When this first significant pirate attack in St. Augustine occurred, Drake was on his way home from his savage raid on Cartagena. When his fleet of twenty-three ships approached the Florida coastline, they noticed a light flickering in the darkness. They quickly identified the light as coming from a Spanish watchtower, which marked the entrance to the St. Augustine Harbor.

While at the outpost, Drake attacked it, destroying the local military fort, stealing money and supplies and burning the buildings. By the time he fled the area, he had nearly destroyed St. Augustine, earning the title of "Sea Dragon."

Unfortunately, the Spanish defenders and townsfolk were outnumbered, forcing many to flee into nearby swamps and marshes to escape. Drake took anything and everything he could find and then burned the city to the ground. This horrific event affected the area and history so much that today, several reenactments are hosted annually in June.

Drake's attack on St. Augustine resulted in the military building a coquina fort, the Castillo de San Marcos, which still stands today. Once this fort was built, the city and surrounding area never fell victim to pirate attacks again.

In 1688, Jamaican pirate Robert Searle set out and captured a Spanish vessel and sailed it into St. Augustine's Harbor. On docking in the harbor, he and his men stormed ashore, overpowering the guards and running rampant through the town. The pirate swarm murdered and pillaged, leaving several children, including a five-year-old girl killed by Searle, among the dead.

According to pirate legend, the spirit of the five-year-old girl continued to haunt Searle until he finally went mad. It is believed the torment he suffered at the hand of the child's ghost led him to kill himself years later.

Historic district, St. Augustine, Florida. *Library of Congress, Carol M. Highsmith.*

Mr. Doughty beheaded by order of Sir Francis Drake, at Port St. Julian, on the coast of Patagonia. *Library of Congress, John Goldar.*

The Spanish built a fort to protect St. Augustine. The Castillo de San Marcos was designed and constructed between 1672 and 1695 to protect the community against the dangers lurking in the seas. Throughout the years, the fort protected residents from pirate attacks and hurricanes.

Castillo de San Marcos is rumored to be one of the most haunted locations in St. Augustine. Although Drake and Searle are not among the ghosts spotted at this location, many visitors have reported seeing the image of a pirate believed to be Drake lurking in the shadows of America's oldest town.

Many spirits haunt the Castillo de San Marcos, including shadow figures and the headless ghost of Chief Osceola. It is unknown if any spirits haunt this fort; there are reports of spirits of Spanish military personnel and other military officials who served at the fort throughout the years, defending the famous fort from pirates and other threats.

The Pirate & Treasure Museum may house many artifacts showcasing pirate lore and history, but it is also haunted by notorious pirates attached to these artifacts. This famous St. Augustine museum displays everything from Jolly Roger flags to pirate gold and treasure chests to weapons. Many employees believe the museum is haunted by the spirits attached to these artifacts and the wandering spirits who make their way to the museum from Ripley's Believe It or Not! across the street. Common paranormal activity in the museum includes unexplainable noises, apparitions and shadow figures.

Since the Golden Age of Piracy, St. Augustine has been threatened by some of the most notorious pirates in history. Today, St. Augustine is still home to many of these pirates, who make their presence known to those who are open-minded enough to witness their existence.

ST. AUGUSTINE LIGHTHOUSE

Today, the St. Augustine Lighthouse is a place to enjoy the beauty of Florida's rich coastal culture and amazing views from the top of the tower. Though the current lighthouse was not built until 1874, records indicate a lighthouse-style structure or watchtower was constructed in the area as far back as 1586. A map from Sir Francis Drake's raid on St. Augustine indicates the presence of a small tower on Anastasia Island.

The map refers to this watchtower as a beacon on the sand hills, which the Spaniards used to watch for and discover ships at sea. It was a coquina

Looking up to the top of the St. Augustine Lighthouse from the base of the outside. *Philip R. Wyatt.*

Looking up the spiral staircase leading to the top of the St. Augustine Lighthouse. *Philip R. Wyatt.*

watchtower similar to others used by the Spaniards to monitor Florida's coastline until the United States acquired Florida in the Adams-Onis Treaty in 1821. Once Florida was part of the United States, the government started to work on its new project to illuminate the peninsula's coastline.[7]

The lighthouse was lit in 1874 after replacing the large Spanish lighthouse, which operated for over 150 years before the Atlantic waves caused it to topple into the waters below.

Even with the Spanish watchtower keeping an eye over the area, the city has a long and tragic history of being attacked by pirates. The first recorded pirate attack on St. Augustine was led by Drake, who, with his two-thousand-member crew, burned the city to the ground in 1586. The next attack was led by Searle in 1668, which resulted in many men, women and children left for dead, including the governor's daughter.

Standing watch over St. Augustine, the lighthouse tower and surrounding land have witnessed many attacks and pirate-related events that have left an imprint on the environment. To this day, many people witness spirits and supernatural occurrences around the lighthouse, which may be connected to the many pirate invasions the city experienced. However, St. Augustine

Lighthouse has seen so much death, devastation and destruction that the pirates are not the only spirits spending time enjoying the view from the lighthouse tower.

CASTILLO DE SAN MARCOS

The raid on St. Augustine by Sir Francis Drake and his men aboard twenty-two ships and the following attack by Robert Searle's pirate crew made the Spanish realize they needed additional protection in the area. Mariana, queen regent of Spain, and her advisors realized that the old wooden forts no longer effectively protected Florida's coast. To increase security and protect citizens in Florida, she approved the construction of a masonry fortification to guard the city.

Construction of the Castillo de San Marcos began on October 2, 1672.[8] The Spanish in St. Augustine needed a defensive fort to protect the town against pirates and English attacks and to protect their Atlantic trade route. Today, the fort is preserved as part of the Castillo de San Marcos National Monument at Anastasia Island as the oldest masonry fortification in the continental United States.

To protect St. Augustine, the strong coquina fort was constructed using oyster shells that were burned by construction workers into lime and mixed with sand from nearby beaches and seawater to make mortar. Spanish for "small shells," the coquina was quarried from the Kings Quarry, located on Anastasia Island across the Matanzas Bay from where the fort was built. The stones were ferried across the bay to the construction site, and workers used pulleys to place the large stones.

Workers were brought in from Cuba to assist the Native Americans from nearby Spanish missions in constructing the fort. Slowly, as construction continued, the walls rose one by one until the near-indestructible fort was completed. The crew took twenty-three years to complete the construction of Castillo de San Marcos, which was finally put to use in 1695.

Because they were unsure if the shell walls would survive against cannon fire, the fort was built with seaside walls that were nineteen feet thick, while all the other walls were twelve feet thick. When construction was complete, the structure was like no other the Spanish had built at the time. It was ready to fight off any incoming pirate attacks, and the giant courtyard was large enough for all citizens to seek refuge inside while under attack.

Top: The imposing Castillo de San Marcos (St. Mark's Castle in English) in St. Augustine, Florida. *Library of Congress, Carol M. Highsmith.*

Middle: Corner tower of the Castillo de San Marcos in St. Augustine, Florida. *Library of Congress, Carol M. Highsmith.*

Bottom: Short cannon at the Castillo de San Marcos in St. Augustine, Florida. *Library of Congress, Carol M. Highsmith.*

View of Matanzas Bay from the Castillo de San Marcos in St. Augustine, Florida. *Library of Congress, Carol M. Highsmith.*

Additionally, the size and construction of Castillo de San Marcos made it strong enough to survive hurricanes, and the materials used would not burn and were guaranteed to be termite-free. The coquina construction style was so effective that the Spanish built a second, smaller fort in the St. Augustine area, Fort Matanzas, which was also never captured when the town was attacked.

The most intriguing thing about the fort is that it is more than three hundred years old, full of history, and home to many spirits who refuse to leave the fort's protection.

Stories about Andrew Ranson continue to spread throughout the St. Augustine area, especially when sharing stories about how he miraculously escaped death by the garrote. His near-death experience by execution may be what is keeping him behind, making his appearance known to all those who visit St. Augustine. Ranson is one of the most famous ghosts known to roam Castillo de San Marcos, living out his afterlife in this beautiful and historic town.

Visitors and locals have reported seeing Ranson's spirit wandering the fort's courtyard, and it has been captured in photos. Other paranormal accounts believed to be tied to pirates and Castillo de San Marcos's military background include strange light anomalies, sounds of cannon fire, men screaming, disembodied voices, unexplained temperature changes and shadow figures.

FORT MATANZAS

The Spanish recognized the vulnerability of the St. Augustine area, especially the Matanzas Inlet. In 1569, a wooden watchtower was constructed to protect the shoreline and the townspeople. The watchtower also served as a way to watch for pirates and other attackers who also identified this way to gain access and attack St. Augustine.

Built in 1742 by the Spanish, Fort Matanzas guarded the inlet about fourteen miles south of the oldest port, St. Augustine. Many believed this inlet could serve as "back door" access to St. Augustine, requiring it be kept safe and secure.

The Matanzas fort was constructed using coquina stone, similar to the much larger Castillo de San Marcos. However, construction was not as easy as it was for Castillo de San Marcos because workers had to fight marshy waters when constructing the long piles that needed to be driven into the marsh to support the weight of the shell stones. Coquina stone for this fort was quarried at El Piñon, a small inlet south of Matanzas.

Throughout the years, St. Augustine suffered from pirate raid after pirate raid, which kept residents and the Spanish military on constant high alert. In addition to military attacks, the area was no stranger to brutal and bloody attacks, torture and total defeat from the swashbuckling invaders.

The inlet is believed to be a significant scene for crucial events in Spanish colonial history. Though the Matanzas Inlet is more than ten miles from St. Augustine's port, it too fell victim to these horrific pirate attacks. One attack was when the Spanish made their opening move in settling a colony in Florida and were responsible for a massacre of French soldiers near the inlet in 1565.

Fort Matanzas, St. Augustine, St. Johns County, Florida. *Library of Congress.*

Left: Fort Matanzas, Saint Augustine, St. Johns County, Florida. *Library of Congress.*

Below: Bird's-eye view overlooking historic Fort Matanzas in St. Augustine, circa 1969. *State Library and Archives of Florida.*

Finally, in 1740, the Spanish started constructing Fort Matanzas as a final attempt to secure their colony and ward off British encroachments on St. Augustine. The fort was finally completed in 1742, thanks to the efforts of enslaved peoples, convicts and additional Cuban troops who were tasked with completing the construction.

The fort served as a way to help protect St. Augustine from attackers entering the area through the Matanzas Inlet for years. At the end of the French and Indian War, the Treaty of Paris gave ownership of Florida to Britain in 1763. However, after the American Revolution, a second Treaty of Paris returned ownership of Florida to Spain in 1784.

Though Spain was back in control of Florida, including St. Augustine and Fort Matanzas, the fort did not receive the tender loving care it needed from the Spaniards to maintain its original glory. Years of continued erosion and consistent Florida rainfall caused the fort to start to deteriorate.

In 1819, Spain transferred Florida to the United States. Since the fort had deteriorated so severely, soldiers could no longer live inside. Ultimately, the United States officially took possession of Fort Matanzas, but none of its military forces ever occupied it.

Today, the fortified coquina watchtower is open for visitors to explore. Visitors feel like they are walking where many famous explorers, including pirates, once walked along the shores and sailed along nearby waterways.

Among the dunes, tidal creeks and marshes a diverse habitat sits, attracting various wildlife, including egrets, which nest in the area and feed on the near-endless supply of fish and crustaceans living in the salt marshes. These areas are also home to many seen and unseen entities that may be tied to local legends of pirate conquests and swashbuckling activity.

Legend claims this historic fort is haunted, but with the name Matanzas, Spanish for "slaughter/killings," there has to be some paranormal activity to accompany the spooky name. Why Matanzas? The fort was named after the 145 Huguenots killed in 1565.

In and around Fort Matanzas, visitors and park employees have claimed to have heard strange noises and disembodied voices and seen shadow figures quickly darting through marsh areas. Another interesting paranormal claim from the fort includes a bright green light that begins under the water near the fort. It turns into a bright white light, breaking the surface with a featureless face and suddenly vanishing.

Other visitors have claimed the surrounding waters have turned blood red as the sun sets, and the sand gets a reddish tint when stepped on or touched, almost as if it is bloodstained.

No one knows exactly who or what is causing the paranormal events reported throughout this area. Still, several locals believe there is a strong possibility the activity is tied to St. Augustine's history with piracy.

Even though there is a bit of uncertainty about who is haunting For Matanzas, several people have claimed to see apparitions that look like soldiers from when the Spanish occupied the state. Additionally, many spirits and paranormal claims share no evidence that can be linked to one particular resident, soldier, pirate or other person who lived in the area.

Florida beaches are covered with ghost crabs, including the beaches near Fort Matanzas. *State Library and Archives of Florida, Dr. David E. LaHart.*

FLORIDA GHOST CRABS

St. Augustine is a haunted city and is known for an extensive range of paranormal encounters with pirates from the past. In addition, the area's many ghost crabs make their appearance known from dusk until dawn on the shores surrounding Fort Matanzas.

When exploring the area, don't be startled when you suddenly see a sand-colored exoskeleton emerging from beneath the sand, moving forward, sideways or in reverse before vanishing beneath the sand.

Since ghost crabs are more active at night, when exploring any Florida beach, especially those in the St. Augustine area, be watchful so as not to step on the crabs or destroy their habitats.

FOUNTAIN OF YOUTH

Another Florida pirate legend associated with Ponce de León is the legend of the Fountain of Youth in St. Augustine. This story of Ponce de León dates back to Easter Sunday 1513, when he discovered Florida. Once he found the state's peninsula, he spent the next decade searching for the elusive Fountain of Youth. During his search, he fought off yellow fever, malaria and local Calusa Indians.

Upon his arrival in Florida, he christened the land Pascua de Florida, "the feast of flowers." Unfortunately, the beautiful land he discovered would be the location of his death. Ponce de León and his men encountered the Calusa chief San Carlos on Ostero Island, which is modern-day Fort Myers. Legend is unsure what happened after he encountered San Carlos; some report Ponce de León was killed and buried there, while others claim his body was returned to either Cuba or Spain.

Unfortunately, Ponce de León's exploration efforts to discover the Fountain of Youth failed because it is believed he never fulfilled his mission of finding it. However, this Spanish explorer rumored to conduct acts of piracy may have been closer than he ever imagined to the Fountain of Youth.

Ponce de León first landed in Florida near where the fifteen-acre Fountain of Youth Archaeological Park sits today. At the site today is a beautiful stone fountain, but original legends claim that the fountain may not have been an actual fountain but a river or a spring. Either way, the site is beautiful and filled with a long history. Though researchers are unsure of how close he was to the location, many reports claimed he was within a short walk of the site along the shores of St. Augustine, Florida.

One interesting fact about Ponce de León and his quest for the Fountain of Youth is that he never wrote about his journeys to find this elusive location in any of his journals, documents or letters. The legend of his

Entrance to the Fountain of Youth Archaeological Park in St. Augustine, Florida. *Library of Congress, Carol M. Highsmith.*

seeking the Fountain of Youth started after his death when other biographers claimed that the search for the fountain was the motivating factor behind his expedition to Florida.

One biographer, Gonzalo Fernandez de Oviedo y Valdes, a Spanish historian and writer, shared details in 1525 that Ponce de León was seeking the Fountain of Youth in an attempt to cure his sexual impotence. This legend is unlikely because Ponce de León fathered several children and was under the age of forty at the time of his exploring Florida. However, the legend of his search for the Fountain of Youth has stuck with him, and the two have been shared repeatedly throughout history.

His desire to find the Fountain of Youth is also believed because of a legend of a mysterious life-giving spring dating back to the time of Herodotus. This spring was rumored to be in various locations from Ethiopia to the mythical islands of Bimini. Ponce de León believed its exact location was in Florida, so he set his sights on making it to the Sunshine State to gain eternal youth.

Many of Ponce de León's writings shared documentation about colonizing the Americas, spreading Christianity and making the determination that Florida was a peninsula instead of an island. Many historians agree he may have been more interested in looking for islands he could profit from instead of seeking eternal youth.

Paranormal activity reported at the Fountain of Youth includes light anomalies, disembodied voices, spectral screams, shadow figures and feelings of being touched by an unseen force. It

Above: Statue of Juan Ponce de León searching for the Fountain of Youth, circa 1900. *State Library and Archives of Florida.*

Opposite, top: Drawing of Juan Ponce de León at the fountain of youth, circa 1850. *State Library and Archives of Florida.*

Opposite, bottom: Fountain of Youth, St. Augustine, St. Johns County, Florida. *Library of Congress, Frances Benjamin Johnston.*

is safe to assume that the Fountain of Youth is haunted, but does Ponce de León haunt it? Since he never made it there while alive, it is doubtful he haunts the location today. Though some have reported seeing his apparition near where he landed on Florida's shoreline, others speculate that though he never found it while alive, he has found it in the afterlife and remains behind to haunt it.

Many paranormal researchers agree that the area surrounding the Fountain of Youth is very haunted, and there are no new ghosts for several of the spirits. The spirits that haunt the Fountain of Youth could be as much as 1,500 years old, and many are believed to be from the Golden Age of Piracy.

St. Augustine Pirate & Treasure Museum

As history has revealed, the St. Augustine area was a prime location for pirates to attack, and the community has many legends dating back to the Golden Age of Piracy. With so many stories to share, there was no better way to showcase what the life of a pirate was like than at the St. Augustine Pirate & Treasure Museum.

Anyone interested in learning more about pirates and seeing artifacts from the era must visit St. Augustine and explore the museum. This museum is exciting and educational and will transport guests back more than three

Replica of a skeleton pirate called a "goonie" at the St. Augustine Pirate and Treasure Museum in St. Augustine, Florida. *Library of Congress, Carol M. Highsmith.*

hundred years to Port Royal, Jamaica, during the height of the Golden Age of Piracy.

Pat Croce, owner of the museum, opened it in Key West and, after five successful years, moved it to St. Augustine. Moving the museum to the oldest city in America was an easy decision because it was a place where pirates, including Sir Francis Drake, Robert Searle and Ponce de León, frequently visited. The area was a prime contributor to colonial America and the history and legends associated with pirates.

One of the most intriguing exhibits at the museum is Captain Thomas Tew's seventeenth-century treasure chest. In addition to the treasure chest,

Top: Matt Frick is not just a costumed reenactor at the St. Augustine Pirate and Treasure Museum in St. Augustine, Florida, he's the curator as well. *Library of Congress, Carol M. Highsmith.*

Bottom: A display at the St. Augustine Pirate and Treasure Museum in St. Augustine, Florida, of West Indies treasures, discovered in 2007, of the sort that were the plunder of buccaneers. *Library of Congress, Carol M. Highsmith.*

the museum is home to the journal of Captain Kidd's final voyage in 1699. Both of these artifacts, among others, could be the reason why spirits are roaming the exhibit halls of the museum. Several theories claim spirits can attach to various artifacts. Still, they can also act as a portal, allowing spirits to come and go, making it possible for them to keep an eye on their most beloved belongings.

There are several reasons why the Pirate & Treasure Museum is haunted, including the spirits being tied to the various artifacts. Former employees have reported that the place is haunted, and they experience strange occurrences throughout their shifts, including hearing unexplainable noises, seeing shadow figures and apparitions and finding that items disappear and reappear elsewhere in the museum.

There are reports that the ghosts of two young women believed to have perished in a fire in 1944 are haunting the museum.

Anything or anyone can haunt the Pirate & Treasure Museum, including the spirits of pirates or others who lived in the area during the many pirate raids. Plus, the museum is located across the street from Castillo de San Marcos, so there is a good chance that a few of the spirits haunting the fort have made their way to the museum to explore the pirate-themed artifacts.

POTTER'S WAX MUSEUM

Potter's Wax Museum is set near the Tolomato Cemetery and is rumored to be haunted by spirits of St. Augustine's past. The museum is home to 160 life-sized wax sculptures that are enough to give anyone the heebie-jeebies. Nothing compares to standing next to what is believed to be a handmade wax statue and turning around to realize it was not a statue but a ghost. Seeing apparitions believed to be wax figures is common at Potter's Wax Museum.

The inspiration behind Potter's Wax Museum came about in 1948, when George Leonard Potter decided to turn his dream into a reality—opening a wax museum. When the museum opened as Potter's International Hall of Fame, it was the first wax museum in the United States and housed more than two hundred wax figures in a two-story building. In 1970, Potter's Wax Museum was recognized as the second-largest wax museum in the world.[9]

After Potter's death in 1979, his family was granted ownership of the museum, and they managed it for a few years before selling a majority

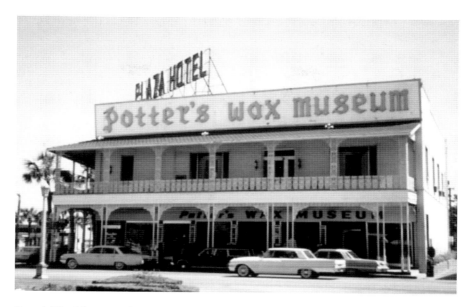

Potter's Wax Museum—St. Augustine, Florida. *State Library and Archives of Florida, D.G. MacLean.*

of the collection. Soon after, Dottie White, the museum's former curator, bought 160 of the remaining figures so she could reopen the legendary wax museum, renaming the museum Potter's House of Wax. The new museum officially opened in 1987.

Immediately upon entering Potter's Wax Museum, guests are greeted by rows upon rows of bottles in the Apothecary Room, which is rumored to be one of the most haunted locations in the museum. Bottles in the Apothecary Room have been known to rattle randomly, with no explanation. Though it is possible the bottles could be rattling to something happening outside, staff have reported rattling at night when there is no traffic outside the structure.

Other paranormal activities reported at Potter's Wax Museum include seeing full-bodied apparitions, which at first are thought to be wax figures, but upon closer inspection, the statue has vanished.

Another one of the more haunted rooms at the museum is the Pirate Room, where many have reported seeing shadow figures darting around the room and dashing back and forth behind the wax statues. Other strange and unexplainable occurrences in this museum room include seeing a strange fog emerge from the floor, light anomalies, disembodied voices and crying sounds. Video and camera equipment have also malfunctioned when near certain statues of this room and then suddenly started working again after leaving the room.

Some people claim the paranormal activity happening within Potter's Wax Museum is a result of the funhouse effect due to all the creepy wax figures. This phenomenon is named for the sensation one gets when visiting a funhouse at a carnival. The series of convex and concave mirrors create a distorted visual effect. The many wax figures set in a small, dark room can have a similar influence on the mind, which may lead to the mind trying to make sense of the chaos in the room.

One of the most eerie displays in the museum is the depiction of Andrew Ranson in the garrote on the day of his attempted execution. Many people have reported suffering from creepy feelings and experiencing strange occurrences near the exhibit. It is unknown if the paranormal activity in the pirate room and near this display is caused by Ranson's spirit, but some people believe he found his way to the museum in the afterlife and makes his appearance known now and then to unsuspecting visitors and employees.

16

YBOR CITY

Ybor City, known for being home to many notorious pirates and, in recent history, home to the Gasparilla Pirate Festival, has a long, haunted history. Named after the pirate José Gaspar, whom some historians believe never existed, the festival attracts hundreds of thousands annually. During the festival, attendees enjoy fantastic food, beverages, live entertainment, vendors and pirate-themed things. It is a must-have experience, and many people come for the pirate festivities and the spirits tied to local pirate legend and lore.

Some spirits hanging around Ybor City are believed to be tied to Gaspar and the many people associated with his pirating and pillaging. However, the paranormal stories depend on which local legend is considered the truth behind Gaspar and his legendary life in the Tampa Bay area.

One legend claims Gaspar began his notorious pirate lifestyle as a troubled adolescent who kidnapped a young girl for ransom. Upon his capture, he decided to go to prison or join the navy. He chose to join the navy and served with distinction for several years until he led a mutiny against his tyrannical captain. Upon winning his mutiny, he took the ship, escaping to Florida.

Another legend tied to Gaspar's pirate roots suggest he was a nobleman who rose in the ranks of the Spanish Royal Navy. He was well respected and became councilor to King Charles III of Spain. He was loved by all until he was wrongfully convicted of stealing some of the royal jewels, and before going to prison, he escaped custody, stole a ship and headed off to Florida.

Upon his final arrival in Florida, after spending decades pirating, he set out to split the loot among his crew. That was, until they spotted a British merchant ship and wanted to get one last score. Unknown to him and his crew, it was not a British merchant ship. Instead, it was the U.S. Navy ship, USS *Enterprise*, hunting pirates in disguise. Knowing they would lose

Tile entryway in Ybor City Tampa Florida. *Library of Congress, Carol M. Highsmith.*

the battle, his crew surrendered, and Gaspar reportedly wrapped the chain of an anchor around his neck and jumped overboard, never to be seen again.

The Florida Brewery (now a law office) and the Cuban Club are considered some of the most haunted places in Ybor City. Many of the spirits are associated with troubled times in the area, resulting in fights, brawls and many deaths. And not all are associated with pirates. However, many locals believe that much of the paranormal activity is fueled by all the pirate activity of the past.

Annual mock invasion of Tampa during the Gasparilla Carnival, Tampa, Florida. *State Library and Archives of Florida.*

17

PENSACOLA

Pensacola's pirate history shocks many people because they don't realize that pirates occupied Florida and Gulf waters as far north as Florida's panhandle. New Orleans is approximately 242 nautical miles from Pensacola, and the Louisiana port city became a vital staging ground for pirates such as Jean Lafitte in the early 1800s.[10]

Throughout Pensacola, pirates used the multiple inlets, bayous and bays as hiding places. Legends claim these waterways provided the pirates with opportunities to bury their treasure under the cover of native vegetation. Rumors dating back to the seventeenth and eighteenth centuries reveal there may be buried treasure on the shores of Perdido Key. However, the shoals in the narrow mouth created a hazardous environment and made entering the bay tricky.

As the Golden Age of Piracy was ramping up, pirates and privateers targeted American, Spanish and British vessels entering the Gulf of Mexico, Caribbean and surrounding waterways. In 1811, Pensacola had its first encounter with piracy when a U.S. gunboat chased the *La Franchise*, a pirate ship attacking vessels along the northern Gulf region. Unable to escape the military ship, the pirates ran aground on Pensacola Beach. Upon landfall, the pirates burned the ship and scattered, disappearing into nearby woods.

Lafitte set his eyes on Pensacola in 1817 and planned to bring a group of pirates from New Orleans to take control of Pensacola from the Spanish. The plan was to turn Pensacola into a base of operations for pirates and privateers, which caused Spanish officials to become worried and call their citizens to arms.

Pensacola faced pirate drama once again when pirates aboard the ship *Carmen* were captured and brought to trial in the newly established U.S. District Court of West Florida. The crew of the vessel was charged with firing on the *Louisiana*, which was a federal Revenue Cutter Service vessel operating off the coast of Cuba.

The men claimed they had confused the ship for a merchant ship, and USS *Peacock* witnessed the attack and pursued *Carmen*. Upon seeing the naval ship, the pirates turned around and attempted to escape. However, the heavily armed naval vessel managed to capture the eighteen pirates, bringing them to Pensacola to stand trial. Their ship was taken to a separate court in New Orleans, and it is believed it was taken to the commanding officer's compound. The verdict of the trial found *Carmen*'s crew not guilty in January 1823.

Along with the rumors and legends that pirates buried their treasure in the waterways of Pensacola, there are whispers among visitors and locals about eerie experiences and the possibility of coming face-to-face with paranormal activity believed to be tied to Pensacola's pirate past. Paranormal activity throughout Pensacola includes hearing disembodied voices, seeing apparitions, witnessing light anomalies and feeling touched and pushed.

Romana Street stretches from Pace Boulevard to the edge of Pensacola Bay through one of the city's oldest areas. Pirates have haunted the city, especially this area, since the town's earliest times. It is believed many of the pirates and their victims remain behind to haunt the city, making spectral appearances and their presence known.

One legend, the Ghost of Romana Street, is believed to be tied to a bloodthirsty pirate. In the 1820s, pirates were roaming the streets when they captured a young couple, killing the man and kidnapping the young lady. Attempting to save her life, she used the large diamond ring she was wearing to gouge the eyes of one pirate, who released her. But before she could run away, the pirate started swinging his cutlass blindly and managed to decapitate the young woman.

Since this incident, people walking along Romana Street, especially after dark, have seen the apparition of the young lady walking headless along the street. A similar apparition has been encountered walking along Government Street and at Lady's Walk on Santa Rosa Island. Many believed this was the same spirit appearing at different locations, attempting to find her head and seek revenge against the pirate who senselessly murdered her.

18

KEY WEST

K ey West was first discovered by Ponce de León in 1521 when he was on his expedition searching for the Fountain of Youth. He named the island Cayo Hueso (Bone Island in Spanish), and this was just the beginning of Key West's long history of dealing with piracy.

Key West has had a long history with pirates and was a base where the Spanish and American military forces operated to free the Caribbean of piracy. The first commander of the West Indies Squadron, James Biddle, was replaced in 1822 by Commodore David Porter to command the vessels of war for the United States in an attempt to suppress piracy.

Commodore Porter established his squadron's base of operations on Thompson's Island in 1823. The island was named for Secretary of the Navy Smith Thompson and was more commonly called Key West. The settlement was declared Allenton, named after Lieutenant Allen, who was killed in a pirate skirmish off Cuba's coast while commanding USS *Alligator*.

With 1,100 sailors under his command, Commodore Porter was an effective leader, capturing many pirates operating in the West Indies. Many have credited Porter with ridding the Florida Keys of all pirate activity or at least pushing the pirates into hiding, operating stealthier than before. Map records indicate ninety-three pirate attacks from May 1818 to August 1825, with only two occurring in the Florida Keys.

The first pirate attack in the Keys was in 1819 against the schooner *Adeline*, which was boarded by pirates and robbed of everything onboard.

The Southernmost Point, Key West, Florida. *Library of Congress.*

The second attack occurred in September 1822 when the brig *Mary Ann* of Boston was boarded by a pirate schooner and robbed of its whole cargo.

Before the elimination of piracy in the Florida Keys, Key West was a hotbed of pirate activity during the Golden Age of Piracy. Famous pirates, including Blackbeard, targeted and attacked Spanish vessels filled with gold, silver and jewels. Blackbeard made his presence known every time a wealthy Spanish vessel made its way through Caribbean waters.

In addition to providing pirates with prime targets, Key West quickly became a recruiting center for pirates and privateers seeking crewmembers to share their spoils. Famous pirates known to have frequented Key West include Blackbeard, Calico Jack, Anne Bonny, Captain Charles Vane and Black Caesar.

Even after pirates hurried away from the Florida Keys, their spirit and legend live on. Today, Key West is a treasure trove for travelers wanting to learn more about pirate history, walk where pirates once operated, and come face-to-face with the spirit of pirates.

Paranormal encounters believed to be tied to the Golden Age of Piracy include the haunting at St. Paul's Church Cemetery. Here, a man in nineteenth-century attire appears as a misty white vapor and then vanishes as people approach. This spirit does not seem evil, but it has startled many who unsuspectingly encounter it.

Another spirit roaming the cemetery is a sea captain best known for taking great pleasure in frightening visitors. This spirit is believed to be tied to the efforts to drive pirates out of Key West and appears angry and ready to taunt all those who approach him. This spirit has also been seen sitting next to his grave during storms with intense, violent winds.

Other paranormal phenomena that could be tied to Key West's pirate history include light anomalies, capturing apparitions in photographs and seeing apparitions walk down the various streets of Key West, including Eaton Street.

EATON STREET

Eaton Street is a popular tourist destination in Key West, and many people claim they visit often and do not see ghosts. Or do they just not know it?

The amount of paranormal activity along Eaton Street is nearly endless, with many more encounters being shared daily. Though not everyone sees the spirits mingling along Eaton Street, many feel the supernatural energy surrounding them as they stroll through the area. Many visitors who have experienced paranormal encounters along Eaton Street have reported feeling someone's hands on their shoulders, and when they turn around, no one is standing behind them. Others felt like an unseen force was pushing them along, like a spirit guiding them.

Other visitors have reported seeing smoke rings when no one in the area is smoking, hearing unexplainable banging sounds and hearing creepy laughing when no one is around. Many paranormal reports demonstrate that the spirits along Eaton Street do not intend to harm anyone; they want to be seen and heard, especially the spirits of pirates and ladies of the night, the most commonly reported apparitions people come face-to-face with.

Many people have reported seeing the spirits of pirates wandering the streets and carrying a wealth of emotions with them, including merriment and anger. However, there is still nothing to fear from these spirits because many believe most of the energy to be residual, as it plays back to what happened during Eaton Street's past. Though a few spirits are believed to be intelligent haunts, the pirate spirits and many of the ladies of the night, will watch as passersby continue about their business. One spirit is known to walk about the living, laughing and having a blast as tourists explore one of the most haunted locations in Florida.

Hiding in the shadows with the pirate ghosts is a more popular paranormal encounter with Ernest Hemingway and Robert the Doll. With many different spirits and supernatural energy filling Eaton Street, there is a high chance visitors will encounter the spirits, even if they do not know it.

19

SHIPWRECK TRAIL

FLORIDA KEYS NATIONAL MARINE SANCTUARY

The Shipwreck Trail is nestled within the Florida Keys National Marine Sanctuary. It is created by a trail of historic shipwrecks that met their end among the coral reefs. Several ships have been buried in the sandy shallows set a few miles off Florida's coastline. This trail, featuring nine sunken ships, tells stories of the past and how dangerous it was to navigate the waters around Florida.

If ship captains could make it past the dangerous shoreline filled with large coral and other hidden obstacles, they had to worry about the risk of being attacked, boarded and captured by pirates.

ADELAIDE BAKER

The *Adelaide Baker* is submerged twenty feet under the water's surface about four miles south–southeast of Duck Key. The remains of the three-masted iron-rigged ship with a reinforced wooden hull are scattered over a quarter-mile square area of what is referred to as Coffin Patches Reef. It crashed on the reef on January 28, 1889, while making the journey from Florida to Savannah, Georgia, carrying a load of sawn timber.

The *Adelaide Baker* was built in 1863 in Bangor, Maine, but had a different name when it first set sail. This ship was originally called the *F.W. Carver*. A seafaring superstition leads many people to believe that renaming a boat is bad luck, which could have contributed to the demise of *Adelaide Baker*.

Another famous shipwreck along this historic trail is the *San Pedro*, a member of the 1733 Spanish treasure fleet. This fleet was caught amid a hurricane along the Straits of Florida before the *San Pedro*, among other ships, sank. This ship is found in eighteen feet of water about one mile south of Indian Key and is the oldest shipwreck on the Shipwreck Trail.

The *San Pedro* was a Dutch-built ship launched on July 13, 1733. This 287-ton ship sank during a hurricane, and its remains were discovered in Hawk Channel in 1960. Several salvage efforts were attempted, and all that remains of the *San Pedro* is its large pile of ballast stones. However, to provide a unique underwater adventure for scuba divers, seven replica cannons, an anchor and an information plaque were added to the shipwreck.

Other ships found along the Shipwreck Trail include the following:

Amesbury
Benwood
City of Washington
Duane
Eagle
North America
Thunderbolt

Many of these ships were intentionally sunk to be used as artificial reefs to help preserve the coastline of Florida and the fish habitats that thrive in reef environments.

Many people ask why there are so many sunken ships in the waters of Key West, and the answer lies in the fact that during the golden age of sailing, more than one hundred ships passed by Key West daily, and the waters in this area were known as some of the most dangerous in the world. Not only did ship captains have to worry about pirates, but they also had to carefully navigate the treacherous waters and the dangers underneath the water's surface. On average, at least one ship a week was damaged and sunk along the Florida reef.

With many sunken ships along the Shipwreck Trail, the area became popular for pirates, who would come to the area to prey on ships stuck along the Florida reef. Pirates also pillaged items from the shipwrecks found along the trail. It is rumored that some of the ships along the trail belonged to pirates who fell victim to the dangers that caused the ships they were looting to sink.

"What the sea wants, the sea will have" was a fatalistic belief. Besides, a sacrifice to the sea gods might placate them so no more of the crew would follow. Some seafarers believed the waters were a living entity that took what it wanted. Some believe that when a ship wrecked, it was no one's fault but the seas. Sea-inspired superstitions could be one of the many reasons there are paranormal occurrences in this area and other areas similar to the Shipwreck Trail.

Though the ships are set under the surface of the water, there are several reports of the area being haunted. Several people have reported strange occurrences in the region, including equipment malfunctions, strange light anomalies and sounds of men yelling. Some people have also reported seeing ghost ships just off the horizon of this area, and upon closer look, there is nothing there.

20

Dry Tortugas National Park

His stories were what frightened people worst of all. Dreadful stories they were—
about hanging, and walking the plank, and storms at sea, and the Dry Tortugas.
—Robert Louis Stevenson, Treasure Island

Dubbed "America's Devil's Island," this tiny tropical national park has a curious history, including legends tied to pirates. Plus, the Dry Tortugas National Park is no stranger to paranormal activity. Visitors worldwide flock to this island national park for an opportunity to walk among the energies of former Fort Jefferson prisoners, such as Dr. Samuel Mudd, who was imprisoned for his role in President Abraham Lincoln's assassination.

The national park is also the site of many tragedies, including deaths at the Marine Hospital Service quarantine station from 1888 to 1900 and the casualties associated with the Spanish-American War. Many people know Dry Tortugas National Park primarily for its well-preserved fort and lighthouse and its role in the growing pains experienced in southwest Florida.

Along with those growing pains, Florida residents, military personnel and travelers often came face-to-face with the pirates who frequented the Dry Tortugas for daily pillaging, trade and other piracy activities.

Long before Dr. Mudd became an imprisoned resident of Fort Jefferson, Spanish explorer Ponce de León once stumbled upon the shores of Dry Tortugas. Fascinated by the abundance of sea turtles, he named the series of islands Las Tortugas (the turtles), and years later, Dry was added to warn that the area lacked fresh water.

Fort Jefferson, Garden Key, Key West, Monroe County, Florida. *Library of Congress.*

Though many of the islands in the Dry Tortugas were not fit for long-term human habitation, the area served as a shipping lane through the Gulf of Mexico. It was believed whoever maintained control of the Dry Tortugas controlled the passage to and from America's heartland. Ultimately, this caused the region to be a significant part of marine history and the focus of many battles. Pirates took advantage of the lonely islands, seeking cover under the overgrown vegetation and waiting for merchant vessels to pass through the area before falling victim to the horrific attacks pirates were known for.

The U.S. Army Corps of Engineers was ordered to construct Fort Jefferson in 1846 to protect the region from pirate and foreign invasion. The Union fort was built using labor from enslaved peoples, and when completed, it took up the entire sixteen-acre Garden Key, one of the more stable islands in the Dry Tortugas. The fort quickly gained notoriety as the place for prisoners of war and deserters during the Civil War, but it has a dark history that dates back much longer.

The Straits of Florida were speckled with Spanish treasure ships transporting travelers, goods for trade and riches between Cuba and Florida. The possibilities of what each boat carried made them desirable for pirates, and the Florida Straits and the Dry Tortugas became prime hunting grounds for pirates looking to board unsuspecting vessels as they made their way through the dangerous waters and coral barrier reef.

After raiding ships and pillaging vessels that wrecked in the area, pirates sought places to stash, store and hide their booty. Many would sink the

Light tower building at Fort Jefferson, Garden Key, Key West, Monroe County, Florida. *Library of Congress.*

treasure underwater in areas challenging to reach, while others did what pirates do—bury their treasure on the shores of the many islands found in the Dry Tortugas.

Though Ponce de León is credited with naming the area, one pirate lays claim to being the most famous pirate of the Dry Tortugas. This pirate is Jean Lafitte, a flagless buccaneer who helped seal Great Britain's fate during the Battle of New Orleans. Lafitte is also one of history's most romantic and enigmatic pirates.

Researchers do not precisely know when Lafitte was born, his place of origin or his final place of rest, but many believe he was born in Marseilles, Bordeaux or Haiti. A journal, believed to have been written by Lafitte, includes Dominique Youx, his brother and trusted lieutenant. Another document believed to be tied to Lafitte shares details about his parents being French aristocrats who died under the guillotine.

Regardless of where Lafitte originated, most recorded accounts agree he was tall and handsome, with hazel eyes, black hair and a black mustache. He is often called the "Gentleman Pirate" and the "Terror of the Gulf." Both names showed how he could be a gentleman one minute and then turn to command an armada of fifty ships carrying more than one thousand pirates on a pillaging rampage.

Lafitte had a quick temper, and though he was known for pillaging, terrorizing and other acts of piracy, he would get angry when called a pirate. To his dying day, reports claim he angrily denied he was a pirate and flew the flag of Cartagena, which was the major port of Colombia at the time during the rebellion against Spain.

Staying true to his gentlemanly actions, Lafitte may have plundered Spanish shipping vessels to sell the contraband to New Orleans and Florida merchants. He always registered and accounted for everything captured with U.S. Customs. His claims with customs included every gem, piece of gold, textile, loaf of bread and so on.

Like other pirates roaming the waters surrounding Florida, Lafitte made many trips through the Dry Tortugas in search of vessels to loot and travel to nearby ports for trading. He was known to frequent local waterways before returning to his island of Barataria, Louisiana.

Many have reported seeing Lafitte's spirit lingering on Seahorse Key. Still, several believe he is responsible for much of the paranormal activity in and around the Dry Tortugas National Park.

Another intriguing legend from Garden Key shares tales of a shipwrecked crew that spent many days struggling to stay alive and fight off invading pirates.

The crew of the HMS *Tyger* was shipwrecked in the Dry Tortugas in 1742 and luckily survived, stranded on Garden Key for more than fifty-six days. While struggling to survive in the desolate landscape of the tropical island, the crew spent their energy fighting off Spanish explorers and swashbuckling pirates who were looking to conquer the island and defeat the stranded sailors.

The crew finally escaped their island prison by improvising boats from what they could find on the island and in surrounding waterways and setting

Fort Jefferson Lighthouse. Florida Garden Key United States of America, 1986. *Library of Congress, Dale M. McDonald.*

sail to Jamaica. After heading out to sea in small boats, the crew spent another fifty-six days sailing seven hundred miles to Port Royal, Jamaica.

Impressively, the crew did not fall to the attacking pirates and explorers, and minimal lives were lost during the ordeal. Only five crew members died between the time of the shipwreck and arriving in Jamaica—the Spanish killed three, and two died of natural causes.

After surviving continual attacks, the crew made an imprint on the area. Several believe they have seen shadow people hiding and darting throughout the island, to the crew and their attackers. Their imprint on Garden Key may have left a residual effect, resulting in a continuous loop of their life on the island as they struggled to fight off their enemies, including the pirates, during those fifty-six days.

Today, Dry Tortugas National Park is home to Fort Jefferson, lots of wildlife and many spirits that linger long after death. This national park is one of the least visited parks in the country, making it the perfect place to visit when looking to encounter something paranormal. The park is quiet, and the spirits are looking to interact. Upon visiting the park, the spirits definitely will make their presence known.

Not all paranormal activity is tied to piracy. Still, among the disembodied voices, shadow people, light anomalies, portals and spooky specters, many believe several of these occurrences date back to when pirates ruled the seas of the Caribbean. If anything, the Dry Tortugas National Park tells us there is more to the Florida Keys and surrounding islands than sandy Caribbean-like beaches, frozen cocktails, rays of sunlight and fun in the sun. There is a dark history behind this region of southwest Florida, rich with pirate legends and lore.

21

THE STORY OF THE PIRATE SKELETON

CARYSFORT REEF LIGHTHOUSE

The Carysfort Reef Lighthouse is a rusted-out bobbing beacon set in the water of the Florida Keys about six nautical miles from Key Largo. Nestled in the middle of shark-infested waters, this lighthouse is a skeletal reminder of how dangerous the seas surrounding southern Florida can be.

Until 2015, the Carysfort Reef Lighthouse was the oldest functioning lighthouse in the United States, operating since 1852. The lighthouse was named after HMS *Carysfort*, a twenty-gun Royal Navy post ship that crashed into the reef in 1770. In 2015, the lighthouse was decommissioned and now stands as a tourist attraction near the Florida Keys National Marine Sanctuary.

Once home to pirates, these waters have a dark history of legends associated with piracy, dangerous reefs and oceanic deathtraps. Today, the lighthouse is a popular tourist destination for snorkelers and scuba divers looking to experience the beautiful coral reef. In addition to braving possible encounters with sharks, visitors risk encountering one of the many supernatural specters believed to haunt the waters under the lighthouse.

One legend coming from the Carysfort Reef Lighthouse is that of a pirate skeleton floating in the water underneath the octagonal structure. One story found online shares an encounter with a pirate skeleton experienced by a maintenance worker assigned to work on the lighthouse.[11]

Sent to the dormant Carysfort Reef Lighthouse, the maintenance worker was dropped off at Key Largo and then taken by boat to the lighthouse.

What was expected to be a quick and easy job turned into a startling and memorable experience.

As he worked on the exterior of the lighthouse, about one hundred feet up from the water's surface, he started hearing strange noises, which he associated with the expanding and contracting of the steel framing due to atmospheric and water temperatures. When the lighthouse began making noises, he whistled to keep his mind busy and focused on the job.

About ten minutes into the job, he heard a large splash below him. He didn't think anything of the splash because large fish have been known to jump out of the water, and waves splash around as they hit the rusted steel structure of the lighthouse.

However, the splashing continued, and he saw no signs of what could be causing the activity below him. He climbed a bit lower to investigate, and when he reached the base of the structure near the water's surface, he peered into the water below. What he saw shocked him.

The maintenance worker claimed to have seen a full-bodied skeleton floating in the water underneath the lighthouse. First, thinking he was hallucinating from being in the sun too long, he poured water over his head to cool off and clear his mind. He then looked at the water, and the skeleton floated by again.

The second time he saw the skeleton,

Top: Carysfort Reef Lighthouse, 1892. *State Library and Archives of Florida.*

Bottom: Snorkeler at Carysfort Reef Lighthouse. *State Library and Archives of Florida.*

he could see all the details. It appeared old, as if it had been decaying for a long time. Some strips of clothing, which looked dated, remained on the

GHOSTS AND LEGENDS OF FLORIDA PIRATES

torso and legs. Suddenly, the skeleton disappeared before his eyes. He said it didn't sink into the depths of the water below; it slowly faded away.

Some reports of this story claim the skeleton was wearing simple clothes the lighthouse keepers would wear in the 1920s, while others claim the clothing resembled that of something a pirate would wear.

There are several reports that the Carysfort Lighthouse is haunted, including those from several people who have encountered the apparition of former lighthouse keeper Captain John Whalton. Some have also reported seeing supernatural entities in the waters below, many reporting that these creatures almost appear mythical.

Whether pirates are haunting the waters surrounding the Carysfort Reef Lighthouse or something else lurks in the dark waters below, those who have visited the lighthouse agree there is something eerie happening at the out-of-service lighthouse.

PART III
PIRATE LEGENDS

22
THE STORY OF
THE FLORIDA PIRATE

First published in Blackwood's *Edinburgh Magazine* in 1821, John Howison's story "The Florida Pirate"[12] has become a relevant piece of fiction shared through generations. Howison was the magazine's most notable and prolific author of tales of terror, and his story tells the story of a ruthless Black pirate captain with a violent past.

The story shares how the pirate captain was battling to overcome the violent oppression he suffered from his past enslavement and emerged as a tyrannical pirate as the United States and European powers were bickering about pressing political questions of the day. The story is a seamless mix of romantic tales, traditional gothic legends and slave narratives, creating a fantastic story loved by readers on both sides of the Atlantic Ocean.

Ultimately, this story shares a tale of piracy and slave rebellion off the coast of Florida. The story starts with the doctor discovering a foreign land on one of the Bahama islands, where he was left broke, in debt, alone and wondering what his next steps in life would be. While lodging in a small town on the island, he spots a schooner and, upon further investigation, discovers the schooner may have belonged to a pirate.

The man takes a small boat lying abandoned out to the schooner, and in the gloom of night, he approaches the larger vessel. As he approaches the schooner, a voice calls out to him, requesting his identity and his need to approach the ship. When he reaches the side of the ship, he asks to see the captain.

Pirate murals like
this one help keep
the legend of
Florida pirates alive.
*State Library and
Archives of Florida.*

Upon speaking with the captain, the doctor says he knew they were pirates and offers his services as a medical attendant on the ship. The captain agrees but declares the doctor will never leave the ship again.

While on board, the doctor notices most of the crew are Black and speak English and French. The men are generally lively, but fights and brawls occur when crewmen disagree.

The pirate captain, Manuel, sends a crewman ashore to collect the doctor's belongings and pay the person he had been residing with. Once back on the boat, they lift anchor and head out to sea. Captain Manuel has a chilling manner with more dignity than the doctor expected based on the Black men he had encountered in the past.

Aboard the schooner *Esperanza*, the doctor does not know where they are headed, and as the land behind them disappears, he is warned not to inquire about their destination. After being at sea for about one week, the ship casts anchor at the mouth of Ibarra Harbor in Cuba to obtain firewood from the riverbanks.

At Captain Manuel's request, the doctor accompanies the men ashore on a night when the weather is clear and calm. The landing party enters the river, slowly rowing through its windings. It is very dark, but the men, excluding the doctor and captain, manage to go ashore and start cutting down wood.

While waiting for the men to finish cutting wood, Captain Manuel begins sharing his past story with the doctor. Though the captain was born in South Carolina, his mother came from the coast of Africa. He was raised as an enslaved person on a large plantation where his mother was a house servant and served their master with more than one hundred others. His mother was treated better than most others because their master, Mr. Sexton, was addicted to the pleasures he received from eating her exquisite cooking.

At the age of sixteen, Captain Manuel started serving his master more officially but eventually was forced to work the fields. Throughout his years at the plantation and having access to the main house through his mother, he heard many conversations Mr. Sexton and other local enslavers had. This event made him believe they were mean, wicked, unjust and cruel, and he felt superior. They also feared the enslaved people forced to work on their plantations would overtake them solely based on the large numbers.

From the time he was a young boy, he was beaten and mentally abused, making him dream of being free. After learning about a free Black man who knew how to read, Captain Manuel started to steal newspapers from his master, eventually learning how to read with the assistance of the older freedman.

After becoming more educated, the captain started to look on his fellow slaves as if they were degraded and ignorant. Seeing how oblivious they were to how life could be and how oppressed they were, he felt pity and disgust.

While living in misery, the captain fell in love with a young girl, Sabrina, an enslaved person on the adjoining estate. He used to sneak away at night to visit Sabrina until Mr. Sexton awoke one night to discover he was missing, which uncovered the entire affair. He was flogged and ordered to remain on the estate while Mr. Sexton complained to the proprietor of the adjoining estate. After the complaint, Sabrina and her mother's hut was burned to the ground in an attempt to remove the location where the young lovers would meet.

Captain Manuel was so enraged over the ordeal he found a way to convince Mr. Sexton's daughter, who was in love with the son of the adjoining plantation's proprietor, to talk to her father about purchasing Sabrina and bringing her to the same plantation so they could get married. Mr. Sexton refused.

One day, young Manuel was asked by Miss Sexton to deliver a message to her lover on the nearby plantation, promising if he were caught, she would defend him. However, he was caught; she didn't protect him and he was severely beaten by Mr. Sexton until he defended himself with his fist, landing the enslaver on the ground. He was convicted of the crime of striking his master, flogged and spent several months in an isolated prison.

Upon returning to the plantation, he continued to serve his master during the day, but at night, he worked with the other enslaved persons to get their revenge against the evil man who lived on the plantation they served. Gradually, they placed combustibles throughout the mansion and plantation in areas that weren't noticeable. Then, one night, they set all of them on fire.

When Mr. Sexton came out of the main house and was greeted by one of his slaves on a horse, those rising against their enslaver jumped out from the darkness, seizing the reins of the horse and grabbing hold of Mr. Sexton. To kill him, Captain Manuel looked into his master's eye, who was pleading for his life. Mr. Sexton would grant him his freedom if he let him live.

Instead of killing their master, the enslaved people tied him to a tree and made their way toward the seashore. It took the group two days to get to the coast, where they stole a boat and headed out to sea. Soon, they met a pirate who immediately took them onboard, where Captain Manuel started learning about being a seaman. They enjoyed sailing the waters and collecting many prizes, but the ship became too well known, and the current ship captain was afraid they would be captured and tried for piracy.

Upon docking on one of the West India Islands, the vessel's captain sold it and paid his crew handsomely. The money Captain Manuel received was enough to purchase a schooner, and he soon became a pirate captain of his ship.

The story about how the captain obtained his ship and crew comes to a sudden end as the landing party returns to the small boat with plenty of firewood. They make their way back to the boat, and at sunrise, they head back out to sea.

While at sea, the doctor observes Captain Manuel having friendly and lively conversations with the crew. The captain spends most of his time on the deck, basking in the sun and smoking a cigar. During their time at sea, traveling from port to port, the doctor witnesses many interactions with the crew, men in the brig and a father with his daughter coming aboard Captain Manuel's ship.

Finally, the crew make it to Matanzas, where they engage in a battle. During the battle, a young officer boards the ship along with his American crew. In a successful attempt to stop the pirates from continuing their attack, the American crew pours water over the gunpowder and, a few hours later, capture the schooner.

Once control of the vessel is in the hands of the American crew, they set sail for Charleston, which they reach in ten days. The pirate crew is immediately jailed, and the doctor is taken into custody. Soon, the doctor is released under the assumption that he was taken against his will to provide

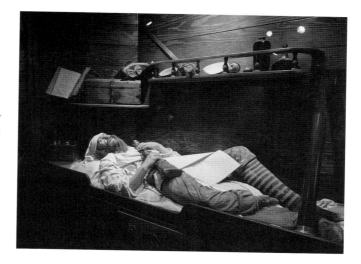

A scary pirate, scary because the figure is not shown as dead but breathing in and out, at the St. Augustine Pirate and Treasure Museum in St. Augustine, Florida. *Library of Congress, Carol M. Highsmith.*

medical attention on board the schooner. Three weeks later, Captain Manuel and seven crew members are condemned to death.

Before the captain's death, the doctor visits the small cell that contains Captain Manuel, whom the doctor feels deserves a better fate. The captain gives the doctor a letter to deliver to Gustavus H. with the instructions to hand over the letter but not to reveal he was sentenced to death.

The doctor starts to immediately search for the letter's recipient, and upon delivering the letter, the doctor is invited to sit down, and he obliges. Gustavus leaves the room and returns with a large bag full of doubloons. Upon handing the bag to the doctor, he claims, "I guess Manuel don't intend that I should be his banker long."

The doctor is shocked that Captain Manuel kept his conviction to be hanged a secret long enough to transfer his legacy to the doctor. The doctor takes the bag and reaches out to Elizabeth, the daughter of the man who boarded the ship during one of Captain Manuel's adventures and suggests they share the loot and go on an adventure together. She obliges, and the two spend the rest of their lives exploring the world.

This story was popular, and since its publication, it has been shared in multiple publications and has inspired many works of literature and film. Like other pirate legends, the Legend of the Florida Pirate is shared by many throughout the state and beyond, keeping the legend alive and intriguing researchers to dive deeper into the history of the Florida Pirate.

A copy of "The Florida Pirate" from the 1820s is available in the archives of the St. Augustine Historical Society Research Library.

23
EVERGLADES GHOST SHIP

A legend in Florida is shared among sailors that dates back hundreds of years. As the legend claims, a pirate ship was picked up by a tidal wave, tossing it deep into the Florida Everglades. It is rumored this ship is occupied by a crew of phantom pirates who are now stranded and left behind to haunt the twisting channels and grasslands of the Everglades.

The story had been shared among pirates and locals living in and around the Florida Everglades. This eerie legend was shared for more than three hundred years before it was picked up and published by newspapers nationwide in 1901.

So, how did these pirates get trapped among the swamps and marshes of the Florida Everglades? According to the legend, the pirates were trapped in the labyrinth of water and grass, eventually dying from starvation. As the pirates died one by one, little did they know that once they died, their suffering was far from being over.

The spirits of these pirates remain behind, still searching for a way to get out of the Everglades. Many people, including Native Americans, hunters

Top: Bog in the Florida Everglades. *Library of Congress, Carol M. Highsmith.*

Bottom: Aerial view of mangrove in the Everglades National Park, 1965. *State Library and Archives of Florida.*

Opposite: Open waters in the Everglades, an ecosystem in South Florida that is unlike any other in the world. *Library of Congress, Carol M. Highsmith.*

and local settlers, have reported seeing a shimmering, misty pirate ship appear with rotting masts and hull. The sails were tattered, and it seemed as if the ship was aimlessly floating in the water, as if the captain was struggling to find a way out of the sawgrass pools.

24

MODERN-DAY PIRATES (AKA TREASURE HUNTERS)

E ver since the first treasure ship crashed off the shores of Florida, Spanish, British and American governments, along with pirates and privateers, set off on missions to retrieve the gold and claim it for themselves; essentially, pirates could be considered the first beachcombers but without metal detectors. Often, the pirates would wait for a storm to roll through the area and then make their way to the beach in search of valuable treasure, which was often washed up on the sandy beaches.

Today, Florida is full of what many call "modern-day pirates." These men and women dedicate their lives to seeking out treasure left behind by pirates and sunken galleon ships off Florida's coastline. Common names of those known as treasure hunters include Mel Fisher, Art McKee and Robert McLarty. Though these modern-day pirates do not go out seeking victims to attack or capture for ransom, the end goal is the same—seek out as much treasure as possible by combing beaches and diving deep into Florida's coastline waters.

Several of the riches discovered by these men are now on display at museums throughout Florida's Treasure Coast. Not only are the displays a magnificent demonstration of pirate history, but they also hold secrets to many spirits who haunt the museums and artifacts held within.

MEL FISHER

Sebastian and Key West

Out of all the shipwrecks throughout Florida waterways, most happened off the shores of the Florida Keys. The most famous shipwreck off Key West's shores, the treasure from the Spanish galleon *Nuestra Señora de Atocha*, is on display at Mel Fisher's Maritime Museum in Key West. This vessel was lost at sea during the 1622 hurricane and was discovered by Fisher in 1985. Items displayed from the wreckage include cannons, navigational instruments, gold chains, coins and silver bars.

Fisher was an Indiana-born former chicken farmer who moved to California to open a diving shop called See Da Sea. He married Dolores (Deo) Horton in 1953 and became a business partner. Horton was one of the first women to learn how to scuba dive and set a women's record by staying submerged underwater for fifty hours. After their marriage, Fisher eventually moved their family of five children to Florida, where he spent decades treasure hunting off the Florida Keys.

Found in Key West and Sebastian, the Mel Fisher Museum is an entertaining venue for learning more about pirates, treasures and shipwrecks. The museum offers visitors opportunities to learn more about pirates, see their treasures and view other pirate-related artifacts collected from throughout the state of Florida and beyond.

Several artifacts Fisher collected and displayed in one of his museums are rumored to be haunted. People who have visited his museum have seen apparitions of pirates, spotted shadow figures lurking in the corners and experienced strange phenomena, including hearing disembodied voices and seeing light anomalies.

ROBERT MCLARTY

McLarty Treasure Museum

Robert McLarty, a retired Atlanta attorney and Vero Beach resident, donated his artifacts from the 1715 Spanish Galleon fleet to the State of Florida, which opened the McLarty Treasure Museum. The museum shares stories about how the fleet of treasure ships met a devastating end and much of the

This page: Looking out onto the Atlantic Ocean from the replicated pirate ship bow at the McLarty Treasure Museum in Sebastian, Florida. *Heather Leigh, PhD*.

riches—silver, gold and copper—sank to the bottom of the Atlantic Ocean off Florida's coast.

All eleven ships sank during the hurricane and were discovered off the coast of Indian River County, which is part of Florida's Treasure Coast. The museum shares the story of the fleet with fantastic displays of artifacts salvaged from the wreckage.

Visitors can watch *The Queen's Jewels and the 1715 Fleet*, an A&E Network production sharing the story of the fleet's attempted voyage back to Spain.

Today, salvagers continue scouring the ocean's floor in search of more of the queen's jewels to recover.

The McLarty Treasure Museum is set on the former site of the Survivors' and Salvagers' Camp from the 1715 Fleet and is now a part of the Sebastian Inlet State Park. Many people claim the land is haunted by an energy imprint on the land and by the artifacts held within the museum. Several strange occurrences reported at the museum include seeing shadow figures and light anomalies, hearing disembodied voices and visitors feeling as if they are not alone when exploring the outside boardwalk headed down to the beach.

Ship's wheel from the replicated pirate ship bow at the McLarty Treasure Museum in Sebastian, Florida. *Heather Leigh, PhD.*

ART McKEE

Thirteen ships from Spain's 1733 fleet were making their way from the New World back to Spain when they encountered a storm off Florida's east coast. *La Capitana*, the fleet's flagship, was among the ships that sank off the Upper Keys. Diver Art McKee started salvaging the vessel's remains in the late 1930s, recovering silver and gold coins, silver bars, weapons, cannons and navigational instruments.

Known as the father of modern treasure diving, McKee was honored for all his Upper Keys treasure discoveries when the items were displayed at the History of Diving Museum. Throughout the years, he also

Top: Art McKee working at the San Pedro Underwater Archaeological Preserve near Plantation Key, 1957. *State Library and Archives of Florida, Andy Harrold.*

Left: Art McKee showing the group the coral encrusted pistol he found, Plantation Key, Florida, circa 1955. *State Library and Archives of Florida.*

Right: Cannons retrieved by treasure hunter Art McKee, Plantation Key, Florida, circa 1900. *State Library and Archives of Florida.*

discovered the *Infante*, *Herrera*, *San Pedro*, *Chaves* and *San José* vessels. The museum set up a remarkable exhibit demonstrating his efforts and the items he found.

Many of the items McKee salvaged could be the reason why the museums where these items are on display report strange occurrences. Several people who have seen items recovered by McKee report strange occurrences, including unexplainable hot and cold spots, the sensation of being touched and sudden bursts of emotional distress.

Whether you visit one of the museums shared in this chapter or any other pirate-themed museum, there is a good chance something paranormal can occur. With the paranormal and legends of Florida pirates, anything can and does happen.

Author's Note

Do not confuse these modern-day pirates with those who continue to commit acts of piracy throughout the world's many waterways. The people referred to in this chapter are solely treasure hunters seeking lost treasure with no intention of attacking or harming anyone.

Modern-day piracy differs significantly from what is being referred to in this chapter and should be taken seriously. Dangerous pirates continue to wreak havoc, attacking vessels of all sizes in the waters of the Singapore Straits, off Peru's coast and around the Horn of Africa. Several reports of piracy have occurred in and around the Florida Keys, especially those manning small boats and yachts believed to have money or something valuable to be seized.

25

PIRATES OF THE CARIBBEAN

WALT DISNEY WORLD, ORLANDO

There is more treasure in books than in all the pirates' loot on Treasure Island and at the bottom of the Spanish Main.
—Walt Disney

No book about pirates and ghosts is complete without mentioning George, known to haunt the Pirates of the Caribbean attraction at Walt Disney World's Magic Kingdom. According to Disney legend, George was a young welder working at Disney on the Pirates of the Caribbean attraction in the early 1970s.

Some claim George was crushed by a beam while working on getting the attraction ready to open, while others say he fell from a tower set in the "burning city" area of the ride. Regardless of how he died, George met an untimely end and it seems he never left the Magic Kingdom.

Cast members report hearing ghostly footsteps when working alone at the attraction, and upon further inspection, they confirm no one is nearby. Additionally, phone calls are made from an empty control room, and when answered, no one is on the other end of the line.

Other paranormal incidents involving George include seeing his apparition appear throughout the ride, but he is mainly spotted hanging around the burning city scene. According to legend, if you see the light burning in the tower of this scene, also known as George's Tower, it means he is present and watching over the ride.

There have also been reports that if someone disrespects George, he will shut down the ride until the person apologizes. Additionally, if he isn't happy with how things are running, he will shut down the ride until he is happy with the park's operation of what many call "his" attraction. Because of this belief, cast members who report to work at the Pirates of the Caribbean attraction say "hello" and "good-bye" to George as they come to and leave work.

Though the legend of George lives on and continues to be passed on from cast member to cast member, Disney has yet to acknowledge George existed officially. Additionally, there are no reported deaths of a construction worker at the Pirates of the Caribbean, especially during its early construction days. So whether or not George was an actual person, the supernatural energy exists today and is wreaking havoc on those who don't believe or disrespect him.

26

PIRATE MYTHS

This book has shared many pirate legends; however, many are based on myths passed down for centuries, creating the romanticized pirate lore we know today. Here are some of the most known pirate myths and whether they are fact or fiction:

Pirates Were Lazy and Fought Only When Needed

Of course, pirates liked to collect treasure with as little effort as possible, but overall, they were ruthless and killed every chance they had to obtain treasure and build the best and most authoritative crew that ever sailed the open waters.

Pirates Buried Their Treasure

Though legend claims pirates buried their treasure to protect it, and it is possible it happened occasionally, pirates didn't live very long, so planning for their future wasn't something on their minds. Since they did not look toward the future, most pirates kept their treasure close to them and rarely buried it in the sand.

Walking the Plank

There is no written record that pirates made their victims walk the plank. Instead, they were known for keel-hauling, which is a method where they would tie their victims up with a rope and drag them under the ship. The result of this option resulted in a fast death from wounds suffered from the dragging or a slow death from drowning. Ultimately, keel-hauling was a much worse fate than walking the plank.

Pirates Had a Code of Honor

Though there was a code of honor among crew mates, there was no generalized code among all pirates. The more ruthless the pirate, the higher the regard other pirates had for him, but that still didn't mean there was a code of honor among any of them. At the first opportunity, a true pirate would betray another if it meant saving their own life or granting them more treasure.

The Most Famous Pirates Were the Best Ones

Many of the pirates commonly known have been captured, tried, convicted and hanged for acts of piracy. The better pirates managed to fly under the radar and never got caught.

Pirates Had a Unique Language

Movies and books claimed pirates would say things like "Arrrr" and "Matey," but this is untrue. Pirates had no particular way of speaking, and what Hollywood portrays as pirates is far from reality.

Women Were Weak Pirates

Women were not weak, and some of the most famous women pirates, such as Anne Bonny and Mary Read, were some of the most notorious. Many females disguised themselves, and it was never known that they were women until they died or decided to reveal themselves to their pirate counterparts.

Costumed participant of the Gasparilla Festival, Tampa, Florida. *State Library and Archives of Florida, Karl E. Holland.*

Pirates Disappeared

There is a belief that piracy ended many years ago. Still, piracy continues today, endangering the lives of many people who take their watercraft of any size out on the open sea. Reports claim piracy causes worldwide losses estimated between $13 and $16 billion annually. Though most pirates centuries ago would murder, kidnap and mutilate victims, pirates today focus on stealing cargo and ships, as well as attempting to collect ransom for wealthy captives.

The Typical Pirate Image

Many Hollywood depictions of a pirate include someone who flies the Jolly Roger, wears an eyepatch, has a parrot for a pet and has a peg leg. Though this image is very likely true, there is little evidence supporting it as a common image of pirates during the Golden Age of Piracy.

27

LEGENDS OF BURIED TREASURE

One of the most commonly shared pirate legends is that pirates would bury their treasure in an attempt to protect it from being taken by other pirates. Though this was not as common as Hollywood and literature would like us to believe, some pirates were known to have buried their treasure on Florida beaches.

One legend claims St. George Island is where treasure hunters can hit the jackpot, especially if they find the buried treasure rumored to be worth more than $6 million. This pirate treasure is believed to have many Spanish gold bars and is buried on the island's eastern tip near Apalachicola.

Though his legend is fictional, José Gaspar's treasure is believed to be near the southern tip of Placida Island. However, this treasure is supposedly impossible to find, mostly because Gaspar never existed and also because it is believed to be hidden in an area known for dangerous water moccasins.

Set in the secret tunnels beneath Fort San Carlos de Barrancas in Pensacola is believed to be a hidden chamber filled with pirate treasure. If discovered, this treasure would provide the finder with more than $3 million in treasure that pirate Billy Bowlegs Rogers reportedly hid. Rogers is rumored to have buried treasure at Bald Point in Escambia County.

Where SR 2 crosses the Chattahoochee River in northwest Florida, a treasure known as the "Money Pit" remains hidden. Though pirates did not find it, Seminole Indians dumped it there to hide about $100,000 worth of gold coins from the occupying British.

Pensacola Bay is believed to hold the secret and entire ship of a Spanish patrol that also contains hidden jewels, gems, gold and silver. Rumor has it that treasure is also buried on Choctawhatchee Bay, St. Vincent Island and Pine Island.

It is possible to walk one of the many Florida beaches and stumble upon a large gemstone or a piece of gold or silver. However, many who head out to the beaches searching for treasure use various

Digging for buried treasure, St. Petersburg, Florida. *State Library and Archives of Florida.*

methods to seek out and collect lost treasure. Some methods used to find lost treasure in Florida include the following:

Metal detecting
Historical research
Shipwreck exploration

What to Do When You Find Pirate Treasure in Florida?

Two boys using a metal detector to find buried treasure, St. Petersburg, Florida. *State Library and Archives of Florida.*

Florida has an extensive history associated with buried pirate treasure and treasure ships sinking off the coastline; many people continue to find treasure that has washed ashore or is buried deep in the sand. But what happens when someone finds treasure while walking or beachcombing Florida's shoreline? Continue reading to learn more about the Golden Rules for Treasure Hunting:

LEAVE NO TRACE: Beachcombers should adhere to the principle of leaving no trace behind, ensuring they do not disturb the natural environment or leave any debris or waste behind.

Three young women uncover buried treasure during the Billy Bowlegs Festival, Fort Walton Beach, Florida. *State Library and Archives of Florida, Karl E. Holland.*

LEAVE BEACHES BETTER THAN YOU FOUND THEM: In addition to leaving no trace, strive to leave beaches better than you found them by picking up any litter or debris you encounter. Participating in beach clean-up efforts can help preserve the beauty of Florida's coastline for future generations.

RESPECT THE ENVIRONMENT: Respect the delicate ecosystems of Florida's beaches by refraining from damaging vegetation, disturbing wildlife or tampering with fragile coastal habitats.

KNOW THE LAWS: Familiarize yourself with all relevant laws and regulations at the local, state and national levels regarding beachcombing, artifact collection and metal detecting. Respect any restricted areas or protected zones.

SAFETY FIRST: Prioritize safety during beachcombing activities by wearing appropriate footwear, sunscreen and protective gear. Be mindful of tide schedules, weather conditions and hazards such as sharp objects or marine life.

LET SOMEONE KNOW: Before heading out for a day of beachcombing, inform a trusted individual of your plans, including your intended location and estimated return time. This ensures that someone is aware of your whereabouts in an emergency.

Get Proper Certifications for Scuba Diving: If you plan to engage in underwater treasure hunting or artifact recovery through scuba diving, ensure that you possess the necessary certifications and training to do so safely. Follow all guidelines and regulations set forth by diving organizations and authorities.

Research Local History: Before setting out on your beachcombing adventure, take the time to research the local history and notable shipwrecks in the area. Understanding the historical context can enhance your chances of finding valuable artifacts and hidden treasures.

Use Proper Equipment: Equip yourself with the necessary tools for beachcombing, such as metal detectors, shovels, sifters and containers for collecting treasures. Ensure your equipment is in good working condition and appropriate for the terrain.

Practice Ethical Treasure Hunting: Practice ethical behavior when discovering artifacts or treasures on the beach. Avoid removing items of historical or cultural significance and report any significant finds to local authorities or historical societies for proper documentation and preservation.

Uncovering buried treasure during the Billy Bowlegs Festival, Fort Walton Beach, Florida. *State Library and Archives of Florida.*

BE MINDFUL OF PRIVATE PROPERTY: Respect private property rights and obtain landowners' permission before conducting treasure-hunting activities on private beaches or coastal areas.

X MARKS THE SPOT! If only it were that easy to seek out and find treasure. Not all Florida beaches are the same, and some places hold on tight to buried and lost treasure, while others are more generous with giving away the loot lost in nearby waterways and beaches. Some of the prime treasure-hunting locations in Florida include the following:

FLORIDA'S TREASURE COAST, encompassing VERO BEACH and SEBASTIAN, is steeped in maritime lore and legend, offering a tempting prospect for treasure hunters. Just off these shores lie the remnants of countless shipwrecks, including those of Spanish galleons and pirate vessels, each potentially concealing untold riches beneath the waves. Adventurers flock to this region, drawn by the promise of uncovering history's lost treasures amidst the sun-drenched beaches and crystal-clear waters.

ST. AUGUSTINE BEACHES, the oldest continuously occupied European settlement in the continental United States, is a testament to the area's rich maritime heritage. Spanish galleons and pirate ships have met their demise here, leaving behind a legacy of hidden treasures awaiting discovery. ANASTASIA STATE PARK and VILANO BEACH are among the favored locales for treasure seekers, where the sands hold secrets centuries in the making.

Farther south, the GUANA TOLOMATO MATANZAS NATIONAL ESTUARINE RESEARCH RESERVE (GTM Reserve) boasts a significant stretch of coastline within PONTE VEDRA BEACH, a haven for ecological enthusiasts and treasure hunters alike. Shipwrecks and buried treasures dot these shores, adding an air of mystery to the reserve's natural beauty.

At FERNANDINA BEACH on AMELIA ISLAND, treasure hunters can explore the historic FORT CLINCH STATE PARK, once frequented by pirates seeking refuge. The island's shores have yielded many artifacts from bygone eras, offering glimpses into a past filled with maritime exploits and buried riches.

For a truly unique experience, adventurers can visit BIG TALBOT ISLAND STATE PARK, renowned for its boneyard beach, where weathered skeletons of oak and cedar trees create a surreal landscape. Amid the driftwood and shifting sands, hidden treasures from centuries past may await discovery, offering a glimpse into Florida's storied maritime history.

Discovering treasure in Florida can be an exciting yet legally complex endeavor. While Florida law prohibits the excavation or removal of artifacts, it encourages individuals who stumble upon such items to document them through photography and report their findings. Cooperation with authorities in documenting discoveries is often welcomed and may involve the finder's assistance.

The finder's rights are contingent on the categorization of the found property. If the property is deemed lost, abandoned or a treasure trove, the individual who discovered it typically has the right to retain ownership unless the original owner makes a claim. This principle follows the notion of "finders keepers," with ownership determined by the circumstances surrounding the discovery.

Metal detecting is generally permitted in Florida without a permit, although it's essential to refrain from causing damage, such as leaving holes. In specific areas like Orange County, where Orlando is situated, metal detecting may require a permit, and any discoveries must be reported to park staff. Historical artifacts or items that are lost or stolen may be subject to confiscation by park authorities.

A cautionary tale underscores the legal complexities of treasure hunting in Florida. While diving off the Florida coast, the Schmitt family uncovered a trove of valuables worth an estimated $300,000. However, federal and state laws dictated that they retain only a portion of their find, with the state claiming a share and the remainder going to the owner of the underwater wreckage site.

Navigating the legal landscape when finding lost property requires careful consideration. It's advisable to contact local law enforcement to understand relevant laws and obligations. Additionally, taking reasonable steps to locate the owner, such as notifying nearby businesses or posting ads, may fulfill legal requirements and mitigate potential legal consequences. Consulting with an attorney, especially for high-value items, can provide valuable guidance and help avoid legal entanglements.

While the prospect of keeping found treasures may be tempting, understanding and complying with the law can prevent legal troubles and ensure a more ethically sound outcome.

When searching for treasure on Florida beaches, finder, beware, because many people believe the pirate treasure is cursed. Though the exact nature of the curse is unknown, and it is not anything like what is portrayed in Disney's *Pirates of the Caribbean*, many who have found and handled pirate treasure have suffered tragic events. These sad events cannot directly be tied to the pirate treasure. Still, like disrespecting Robert the Doll in Key West, several unfortunate events have been linked to people who have picked up a pirate coin or other related artifacts.

NOTES FROM THE AUTHOR

This book encompasses only some of the tales and folklore surrounding Florida pirates. It overlooks the lives many of these pirates led before and after their time in Florida, which may need to be covered in its pages. This book intentionally excludes some hauntings at these sites because it primarily focuses on the paranormal occurrences linked with pirate lore. To delve deeper into the haunted sites featured here, I recommend exploring my other publications, *Haunted Florida Lighthouses* and *Haunted Florida Ghost Towns*.

One more note:

As we delve into the intriguing tales of Florida pirates and their legendary exploits, we must acknowledge the stark realities of modern-day piracy that persist throughout the world's waters. While the swashbuckling adventures of historical pirates may seem romanticized in retrospect, contemporary piracy presents a far graver and more menacing threat.

Modern-day piracy manifests in various forms, ranging from opportunistic attacks on commercial vessels to organized criminal enterprises. These acts of maritime piracy occur in regions known for their economic significance and are of strategic importance, such as the Gulf of Aden, the South China Sea and the waters off the coast of West Africa.

The risks and dangers associated with modern piracy are manifold. Crew members and passengers aboard ships face the terrifying prospect of armed assailants boarding their vessels, often with intentions of theft, kidnapping or even violence. Piracy incidents can result in profound psychological trauma, physical harm and loss of life. Moreover, maritime piracy disrupts global trade routes, imperiling individual seafarers, international commerce and economic stability.

Navigating through pirate-infested waters demands meticulous planning, vigilant surveillance and adherence to strict security protocols. Ship owners, maritime authorities and governments worldwide collaborate to combat piracy through enhanced surveillance, armed escorts, and international legal frameworks. Yet despite these efforts, the threat of piracy persists, reminding us of the ongoing challenges in safeguarding maritime security.

In recounting the tales of Florida pirates, let us remember the stark reality of modern-day piracy, a perilous phenomenon that continues to haunt the seas. May our exploration of these legends serve as a poignant reminder of the enduring struggle to confront and overcome the dangers that lurk on the high seas.

For an up-to-date report about pirate attacks, visit the websites of ICC Commercial Services (https://www.icc-ccs.org/index.php/piracy-reporting-centre/live-piracy-report) and learn more about piracy and how to report it at the U.S. Department of State website (https://travel.state.gov/content/travel/en/international-travel/emergencies/internl-maritime-piracy-robbery.html).

Remember, if you see something, say something, and we will all be safer while enjoying a day out on the water.

Stay safe,
Heather Leigh, PhD

Notes

1. "Chamber Enlivened by Whiskey Creek," *Fort Myers News-Press*.
2. Montgomery, "Chasing Gaspar."
3. D'Ans, "Legend of Gasparilla," 5.
4. Morgan, "Tampa Family Finds a Good Pirate Story."
5. Lambertsen, "Box Found in Tampa Attic."
6. Ibid.
7. St. Augustine Lighthouse & Maritime Museum, "Lighthouse History Pre-1874."
8. Mailing address: 1 South Castillo Drive Saint and FL, 32084, Phone: 829-6506; National Park Service, "Castillo de San Marcos National Monument."
9. Potters Wax Musuem, "St. Augustine Museums."
10. Visit Pensacola, "Pirates in the Pensacola Bay Area."
11. Southern Most Ghosts, "Carysfort Reef Lighthouse."
12. Early Visions of Florida, "John Howison."

BIBLIOGRAPHY

D'Ans, André-Marcel. "The Legend of Gasparilla: Myth and History on Florida's West Coast." *Tampa Bay History* 2, no. 2 (1980): 1–25. https://digitalcommons.usf.edu.

Dry Tortugas National Park. "The Curious History of Dry Tortugas National Park." www.drytortugas.com.

Early Visions of Florida. "John Howison, 'The Florida Pirate.'" https://earlyfloridalit.net.

Explore Southern History. "Ghost Ship of the Everglades—Florida." www.exploresouthernhistory.com.

Florida Division of Historical Resources. "Underwater Archaeology." https://dos.fl.gov.

Fort Myers News-Press. "Chamber Enlivened by Whiskey Creek, Pirate History." November 8, 1949.

Lambertsen, Kristen. "Box Found in Tampa Attic Has Coins, A Map, A Hand and a Mystery." WFLA-TV, April 28, 2015.

Lyons, Douglas C. "Legend of Black Caesar Haunts the Florida Keys." Florida Rambler. February 7, 2024. www.floridarambler.com.

Heath, Charles, and Charles P. Fessenden. "The Florida Pirate." In *The Cabinet: A Collection of Romantic Tales; Embracing the Spirit of the English Magazines*. New York, Fessenden, 1836.

Hernando Sun Staff. "Florida Gulf Coast Golden Age of Piracy." *Hernando Sun*, August 25, 2018. www.hernandosun.com.

Manucy, Albert C. *The History of Castillo de San Marcos & Fort Matanzas: From Contemporary Narratives and Letters*. Washington, D.C.: U.S. Department of the Interior, 1943.

Maxwell, Bill. "Maxwell: Fort Jefferson's Maritime Legacy." *Tampa Bay Times*, October 30, 2015. www.tampabay.com.

McGreevy, Nora. "The True History and Swashbuckling Myth behind the Tampa Bay Buccaneers' Namesake." *Smithsonian Magazine*, February 4, 2021. www.smithsonianmag.com.

Mitch, Captain. "Everglades Airboat Tours | Airboat Fast Facts." Captain Mitch's Everglades Airboat Rides. March 13, 2015. www.captainmitchs.com.

Montgomery, Ben. "Chasing Gaspar." *Tampa Bay Times*, January 24, 2014.

Morgan, Philip. "Tampa Family Finds a Good Pirate Story in the Attic." *Tampa Bay Times*, April 28, 2015.

National Park Service. "Castilo de San Marcos National Monument (U.S. National Park Service)." www.nps.gov.

———. "Ghost Crabs." www.nps.gov.

Nightly Spirits. "The Sulphur Springs Water Tower." July 17, 2020. https://nightlyspirits.com.

NPS History eLibrary. "Fort Matanzas." http://npshistory.com.

Old City Ghosts. "The Haunting of St. Augustine Lighthouse—Old City Ghosts." https://oldcityghosts.com.

Potters Wax Museum. "St. Augustine Museums | St. Augustine Attractions." www.potterswaxmuseum.com/.

Reigelsperger, Diana." Pirate, Priest, and Slave: Spanish Florida in the 1668 Searles Raid." *Florida Historical Quarterly* 92, no. 3 (2013).

Roberts, Elizabeth, Norma Roberts and Bruce Roberts. *Lighthouse Ghosts*. Lanham, MD: Rowman & Littlefield, 2015.

Salustri, Cathy. "Road Trip: The Headless Pirate of Seahorse Key." Creative Loafing Tampa Bay. www.cltampa.com.

Southern Most Ghosts. "Carysfort Reef Lighthouse." https://southernmostghosts.com.

Spectrum News Staff. "The Man behind Gasparilla: Who Was José Gaspar?" Spectrum News. https://baynews9.com.

St. Augustine Pirate & Treasure Museum. "St. Augustine Pirate & Treasure Museum." www.thepiratemuseum.com.

Tampa Bay Newspapers. "The Mysterious History of John Levique Lives in Legends." TBNweekly. June 13, 2006. www.tbnweekly.com.

Timoti's. "The History of Pirates in Florida." April 1, 2022. www.timotis.com.

Treasure Island, Florida. "City of Treasure Island." www.mytreasureisland.org.

True, David. "Pirates and Treasure Trove of South Florida." www.ltrr.arizona.edu.

USA Today. "History of Treasure Island, Florida." https://traveltips.usatoday.com.

Visit Pensacola. ""Pirates in the Pensacola Bay Area: Fact or Fiction?" www.visitpensacola.com.

Williams, Daniel. "Refuge upon the Sea: Captivity and Liberty in 'The Florida Pirate.'" *Early American Literature* 36, no. 1 (2001): 71–88.

Williams, Starlight. "This Tiny, Tropical National Park Has a Curious History." National Geographic, May 6, 2020. www.nationalgeographic.com.

ABOUT THE AUTHOR

Heather Leigh Carroll-Landon, PhD, started her journey in the paranormal field as a teenager after multiple interactions with her grandfather, who passed away many years before. She has researched and traveled to locations to learn more about the history of the land, buildings and local area and paranormal claims. As long as she has been interested in the supernatural, Heather Leigh has been a freelance writer, writing for several newspapers, magazines and online publications. She and her family (Exploration Paranormal) appeared in *Real Haunts: Ghost Towns* and *Real Haunts 3*, where they explored many southern Nevada ghost towns and she has appeared on *Ghost Adventures: Lake of Death*.

She is an author of articles and books and a lecturer about all things paranormal. Her first book, *Haunted Southern Nevada Ghost Towns*, was published by The History Press in August 2022 and her second book, *Ghosts and Legends of the Vegas Valley*, was also published by The History Press in February 2023. These books were followed by her most recent books, *Haunted Florida Lighthouses*, which was published in September 2023 and *Haunted Florida Ghost Towns* which was published in March

2024. Her latest book, *Haunted Florida Roadside Attractions,* recently released in August 2024. She has many more book ideas in the works and hopes to bring them to life in the near future.

She holds a Doctor of Philosophy degree in Metaphysical and Humanistic Science with a specialty in Paranormal Science. She is a Certified Paranormal Investigator and a Certified EVP Technician. She aims to help others take a more scientific approach to paranormal investigations and research.

Heather Leigh is also the founder of Exploration Paranormal, she hosts Exploring the Paranormal and co-hosts Ghost Education 101 with Philip R. Wyatt and Passport to the Paranormal with Joe Franke. You can find Heather Leigh on Facebook (@DrHeatherLeigh), where you will find additional information, including upcoming classes, lectures and more. Or via her websites, www.heatherleighphd.com and www.explorationparanormal.com.

FREE eBOOK OFFER

Scan the QR code below, enter your e-mail address and get our original Haunted America compilation eBook delivered straight to your inbox for free.

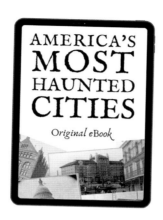

ABOUT THE BOOK

Every city, town, parish, community and school has their own paranormal history. Whether they are spirits caught in the Bardo, ancestors checking on their descendants, restless souls sending a message or simply spectral troublemakers, ghosts have been part of the human tradition from the beginning of time.

In this book, we feature a collection of stories from five of America's most haunted cities: Baltimore, Chicago, Galveston, New Orleans and Washington, D.C.

SCAN TO GET
AMERICA'S MOST HAUNTED CITIES

Having trouble scanning? Go to:
biz.arcadiapublishing.com/americas-most-haunted-cities

Visit us at
www.historypress.com